Your Life and

ɔn Curriculum:

"Highly recommended for teachers, students, and health professionals."
—Larry Payne, PhD, Co-author of *Yoga for
Dummies, Yoga Rx,* and *The Business of Teaching Yoga*

"Robert Butera's book is the first one I have seen that puts the different methods into perspective, and hence helps the student begin to sort out which approach is best for them…This has been immensely helpful in my own practice and understanding."
—John Kepner, Executive Director of the
International Association of Yoga Therapists

"You could have no better guide through the six major meditation styles than master Yogi and scholar Robert Butera. Whether you teach meditation or are taking your first step into practice, this book belongs by your cushion!"
—Amy Weintraub, MFA, ERYT-500,
Founder of LifeForce Yoga Healing Institute, Author
of *Yoga for Depression* and *Yoga Skills for Therapists*

"Students tell us that the Dr. Butera's non-dogmatic philosophy helped to remove fears about meditation. They were motivated to practice regularly and as a result found deeper peace, improved mood, and healthier relationships in everyday life. Students appreciate the personalized approach."
—Erin Byron, Director of the Welkin YogaLife
Institute, Brantford, Ontario, Canada

Meditation
for your
Life

About the Author

Robert Butera, MDiv, PhD, has studied meditation and yoga since 1984. He founded the YogaLife Institute of Devon, Pennsylvania, where he trains yoga instructors, yoga therapists, and publishes *Yoga Living Magazine*. His advanced degrees are from the Yoga Institute of Mumbai, India, Earlham School of Religion, and California Institute of Integral Studies (1998). A lifelong yoga instructor having just one career, Bob opened the YogaLife Institute after completing his PhD. Author of *The Pure Heart of Yoga: 10 Essential Steps to Transformation* (Llewellyn, 2009), he has also trained more than 750 yoga teachers in programs in Pennsylvania, Exeter, New Hampshire, and Brantford, Ontario. Go to www.MeditationForYourLife.com for free video clips.

To Write to the Author

If you wish to contact the author or would like more information about this book, please write to the author in care of Lllewellyn Worldwide, and we will forward your request. Both the author and the publisher appreciate hearing from you and learning of your enjoyment of this book and how it has helped you. Llewellyn Worldwide cannot guarantee that every letter written to the author can be answered, but all will be forwarded. Please write to:

Robert Butera
℅ Llewellyn Worldwide
2143 Wooddale Drive
Woodbury, MN 55125-2989

Please enclose a self-addressed stamped envelope for reply,
or $1.00 to cover costs. If outside the USA, enclose
an international postal reply coupon.

Many of Llewellyn's authors have websites with additional information and resources. For more information, please visit our website at: www.llewellyn.com.

Meditation
for your
Life

Creating a Plan
that Suits
Your Style

Robert Butera, PhD

Llewellyn Worldwide
Woodbury, Minnesota

FIRST EDITION
Second Printing, 2012

Book design by Bob Gaul
Editing by Laura Graves
Cover art: Stones © iStockphoto.com/Angelo Gilardelli
         Sky © BrandXPictures
Cover design by Ellen Lawson
Interior art: Chakra illustration © Llewellyn Art Deparment
         Stones: © iStockphoto.com/Angelo Gilardelli

Llewellyn Publications is a registered trademark of Llewellyn Worldwide Ltd.

Library of Congress Cataloging-in-Publication Data
Butera, Robert, 1964–
  Meditation for your life: creating a plan that suits your style/
Robert J. Butera.—1st ed.
    p. cm.
  Includes bibliographical references.
  ISBN 978-0-7387-3414-9
    1. Meditation. I. Title.
  BL627.B88 2012
  158.1'2—dc23
                    2012016249

Llewellyn Worldwide Ltd. does not participate in, endorse, or have any authority or responsibility concerning private business transactions between our authors and the public.
  All mail addressed to the author is forwarded, but the publisher cannot, unless specifically instructed by the author, give out an address or phone number.
  Any Internet references contained in this work are current at publication time, but the publisher cannot guarantee that a specific location will continue to be maintained. Please refer to the publisher's website for links to authors' websites and other sources.

Llewellyn Publications
A Division of Llewellyn Worldwide Ltd.
2143 Wooddale Drive
Woodbury, MN 55125-2989
www.llewellyn.com

Printed in the United States of America

Contents

Part III: Six Types of Meditation

Part IV: Sustaining a Meditation Practice

Part V: Resources Along the Way

Acknowledgments

This book is a tribute to all who have cared for me and shared their knowledge with me throughout the years. It is with the humblest gratitude that I thank and honor all of their unique gifts and contributions.

First, my wife, Kristen, who is more loving and supportive than words can possibly express. My parents, who had faith in me, didn't force me into a "rational" profession, and supported my decision to travel and study in Asia and India as a young adult. For my grandfather, who meditated every night with his rosary and taught me the values of perseverance and honoring the cycles of nature.

For all my teachers in Japan and Taiwan where I first learned to meditate, in particular the Friends World College, the Ittoen Community, the Naikan Psychotherapy Community, Yamagishi Kai, and Mr. Sakai Sensai.

To my Gurus at the Yoga Institute, Mumbai, India; in particular Dr. Jayadeva and Hansaji Yogendra who gave me a highly sophisticated and individualized training in yoga, yoga therapy, and meditation.

For all of the members of the Society of Friends, especially those at the Earlham School of Religion in Richmond, Indiana, where I did my masters in divinity.

To the dedicated members of the California Institute of Integral Studies who illuminated my PhD studies, especially Dr. Yi Wu, Dr. Jim Ryan, Dr. Paul Schwartz, Dr. Rick Tarnas, and Dr. Rina Sircar.

To all of the Meditation for Your Type program participants and teachers for their feedback, dedication, and tireless efforts on behalf of Yoga & Meditation, especially Erin Byron, Julie Rost, Brian Serven, and Tina Devine.

For my aunt, Marge McDonald, whose experience as an author helped me release my first published book, *The Pure Heart of Yoga*. To the editors Vesela Simic and Joshua Rusbuldt for their patience and insightful comments, and for the folks at Llewellyn Worldwide, including Angela Wix and her team, for making this book reality.

Introduction

One time in India, a mentor made a comment to the effect that it was such a long journey to make halfway around the world to learn such simple principles. Those words did not make sense to the twenty-five-year-old me who loved the adventure of foreign travels and the exotic exploration of ancient cultures. Today, his point makes sense: you do not have to travel around the world to learn how to quiet your mind. You may work, care for the family, and attend to responsibilities all the while focused on self-inquiry and inner peace.

This book systematizes steps a beginner travels in developing a meditation practice. It includes a lifestyle program based on the individual meditator's needs. I have evaluated my journey and those of hundreds of my students to develop this manual in meditation, which will help you establish a personalized meditation practice and lifestyle. This book will guide you to discover what you need to work on by asking you to consider key questions. I do not prescribe one way for everyone; rather, you fill in the blanks to create your own program.

My goal here with you is to be as transparent an author as I can be, sharing my experiences to further illustrate the inclusive and individualized approach of meditation for your type—including the likelihood that over time you may change the way you practice.

This book highlights key teachings for anyone who desires more focus and peace of mind. The goal is to pass on two fundamental lessons: *(1) it is possible to find a type of meditation practice that suits your personality for one to two quiet sittings a day, and (2) sitting silently in a meditation posture is only a small part of what I term the "meditation lifestyle," which is necessary for a successful and enduring practice.* In other words, in order for "just sitting there" to make a difference in your life, the rest of your life must support that focus and peace. The good news is that any step you take in the direction of peace of mind is a step in the right direction!

How This Curriculum Came to Be

The first outline for this book began when I was asked to write a twenty-page essay for a meditation course during my doctoral studies in yoga therapy in 1994. Meditation was a key aspect in the yoga therapy dissertation. The basic definition of meditation is a method to focus the mind, but that understanding does not fill twenty pages. Out of hundreds of books, my research focused on twenty-five, stacked high on the library table where I worked. The task was daunting—what could be said that had not already been written?

Inspiration abounded while reading Daniel Goleman's book *The Meditative Mind: The Varieties of Meditative Experience,* in which he surveys the world's major meditation paths. At that time, there were few books like this. Goleman explained the process of consciousness as it develops through eleven different types of meditation. I decided to categorize the many types of meditation in my essay. After much research and a few heated debates with colleagues about the world's meditation traditions, the summary of six major types of meditation are as follows:

1. Breath

2. Visualization

3. Mantra

4. Devotion, Prayer, or Intentionality

5. Mindfulness

6. Contemplative Inquiry

The Five Goals of This Five-Part Book

While there are many different types of meditation practice, one must be leery of believing that there is one premier method. If there were indeed one best form, most meditators would have discovered it by now. The reality is that everyone is unique, and each of us will take to different styles in his or her own way. This book redefines the claim that one path of meditation is most effective by adding three words to that notion: "for your type." *Meditation for Your Life* will introduce you to a variety of meditation practices and ultimately enable you to discover which practice best suits your personality and lifestyle.

Goal #1: Part I of this book presents definitions of meditation, examples from my life and others, and a set of exercises to help you consider your natural predisposition and experience with meditation. Students new to meditation continue to impress me with their natural, intuitive self-understanding. Take the time to journal your thoughts. Knowing your past tendencies will give you valuable information for moving forward with one type of meditation instead of another. Setting reasonable expectations as well as determining your personal goals starts your journey with clarity.

Goal #2: An essential part of establishing your own meditation practice is learning about and integrating a meditative lifestyle. Quieting the mind through your lifestyle will support your "success" with formal meditation. Just imagine the effect on the mind if you are yelling at other drivers on your commute home from work and then arrive home to sit down to practice! There are stages to quieting the mind, and part II of this book will introduce the benefits of eating right, physical exercise, positive thinking, and stress reduction. You can practice meditation without attending to these elements, but the inherent challenges you'll face will likely cause you to stray from the practice—or worse yet, be counterproductive when you do sit down to practice. Once you begin to integrate supportive lifestyle changes into your daily life, however, you may well begin to feel as though you are meditating even in the midst of everyday activities. Your lifestyle plays a part in reducing stress and increasing composure.

Goal #3: The explanations and practices in this book will help you identify from the six major methods the type of meditation that suits your unique personality. You can discover the method that works best for you through trial and error. To my knowledge, there are no tests that can assess the most effective meditation practice for an individual. The introduction to various meditation methods this book provides will save you the time and money of attending seminars and classes in styles that may not resonate with you. When you have discovered the method that works for you, how far you wish to take your practice is, of course, up to you.

Goal #4: After you have discovered the meditation method for your type, the next hurdle most new meditators are not aware of is the challenge of sustaining the practice over time. The new practitioner's enthusiasm for meditating begins to clear the cobwebs of the mind, but the dog days emerge soon enough. The novelty of discovering a healthy lifestyle eventually becomes your daily routine, and the fascination of experimenting with the six major types of meditation gives way to the discipline of working with one method that suits you. Soon you begin to notice that unresolved karma or unresolved psychological issues surface during meditation. Because the mind is becoming less distracted with regular practice, haunting internal issues will become apparent to even the most balanced person. This book will examine the reasons for avoiding meditation practice and in so doing, prepare you to go the distance. Consult any longtime meditator, and you will hear the many reasons the mind begins to produce at this stage to avoid meditating. Although the mind may resist, it is your task to overcome this resistance and to reap the benefits of persistence.

Goal #5: You may well be inspired to go deeper along your meditation path, which is why this book introduces you to resources that will begin to help you find a meditation group to support your growth. For thousands of years, meditators have found support and guidance by meditating with one another. You too may find yourself drawn to a community of support.

Getting to Know Your Author

As a friendly guy with a big heart, I want to let you know that the motivation for writing this book is to make the meditation process easier for you. I say this in the book: meditation is tough—facing your deepest insecurities, while great once your painful, limiting beliefs are released, it just ain't easy doing the releasing. However, growing *is* possible, and the joy on the other side of overcoming your pain is glorious!

We all come to meditation from different paths; none are right and none are wrong. Before you dive into this book's material, let me fill you in on my background and how I came to understand this topic. If I include my childhood religious upbringing, by the age of twenty, I had been exposed to the six major types of meditation, presented in this book. As a carefree and idealistic college student, I learned meditation for three years in Japan, one year in Taiwan, and six months in India during a daily yoga and meditation intensive at an ashram. Time was on my side: I was young, *and* I could give all my time to this endeavor. Instructors were very accepting; they honored my self-discovery process and helped me find my way. It was understood that a person's path would be years in the making, so there was no rush and no push to follow one path and not another.

In its most accepting form, I found the study and practice of meditation were understood as an inquiry that must ultimately suit each individual's disposition. This point was made especially clear when I learned meditation in the yoga tradition, where the guru, who knows all forms of meditation, teaches each student a form appropriate to his or her disposition. Having experienced this open-minded approach firsthand, I want to pass this inclusive and broad-minded view of meditation on to you.

Learning in monasteries, I found the study of meditation simple because no one was trying to push one method over another. After returning to the States, I completed a doctorate in philosophy and religion. Meditation was also a fundamental part of my studies at the California Institute of Integral Studies as mentioned above.

This same point of personalizing spiritual practice is emphasized in my first book, *The Pure Heart of Yoga: Ten Essential Steps to Transformation* where I highlight the inner process that occurs when a person performs yoga postures. Discovering your personal yoga posture routine and personal intention is highlighted in that book. And that routine may change over time. A second main point related to yoga that is discussed in this book is the importance of preparing the mind and body for meditation. While yoga practice may be used for fitness and health, another purpose of yoga poses, breathing, and relaxation is to prepare the mind for meditation. Rather than diving into the stillness of meditation, practicing some basic yoga and breathing along with relaxation softens the transition from a busy life to a tranquil meditative state.

Throughout the book are various case studies or short meditation stories included for one reason: I want you to know that everyone can meditate. The paradox with meditation practitioners is that you are only really good at meditation when you are able to be as normal a person as everyone else, all the while knowing profound wisdom about yourself and humanity as a whole. I want you to join me in these two attributes. If you are already there, I hope to give you some more tools to enhance your meditation practice, keeping you in a place of happiness and joy!

Two Disclaimers

Although major meditation groups will be noted throughout this book, it is not possible to list all of the meditation groups available to readers; there are far too many! It is up to you to make the effort to find a local meditation class or group, as well as a mentor. You may have to experiment with various groups or classes until you find a supportive learning situation. Those of you who belong to religious organizations may find or form a group within that organization. The personal rapport you experience will be far more important than the denomination, name, or prestige of the meditation group itself.

Also, bear in mind that it is possible to meditate with a group that does not practice the type of meditation you practice and still benefit. For example, if you are a visual practitioner and tend to visualize a teacher's instructions in a breathing meditation class, that is perfectly acceptable. Ultimately your difficulties with meditation will be on a more psychological level, in terms of your motivation for daily practice or the common difficulty of accepting repetitive thoughts. This is why a personal relationship with a local meditation teacher—someone who knows you and cares about you as a human being—is a most profound benefit to your practice. A single half-hour conversation with a high-profile meditation teacher may not be worth a year's worth of five-minute chats with a teacher who knows you well. Again, you will have to make the effort to find the right mentor for yourself.

Part I

*Beginning Your
Meditation
Journey*

The purpose of these early chapters is to present the kinds of problems people usually encounter at the beginning of their meditation journey. First attempts to meditate leave many feeling as if it did not work. In this section, you will be guided to examine your motivations and expectations and to understand that all efforts are "successful." You will also begin the process of learning about yourself in relation to a type of practice. Throughout the book, I will emphasize that an important shift occurs when a practitioner stops focusing on following a method and begins focusing on practicing for peace of mind.

The first three chapters include important journaling exercises concerning your past, present, and future. Responding to these questions by writing in a journal is important. Writing focuses the mind in a way that simply thinking or remembering abstractly does not. Recording your responses also allows you to refer back and learn from them later.

In chapter 1 you will be asked to unabashedly write down your wildest wishes for the future in relation to meditation—prior to a discussion and examination of assumptions, expectations, and misconceptions about meditation. Quieting the mind is no simple task, and your endeavor will benefit from the information you acquire in chapter 2 when you dive into your memory to identify activities that have calmed you in the past. In chapter 3, we will examine your present-day life to identify and maximize the good things you already practice to center and balance yourself. You may discover that you want to increase or renew your commitment to some of these things.

One

....

Expectations, Assumptions, and Misconceptions about Meditation

As meditation becomes more popular in mainstream culture and the scientific community continues to document its benefits, more and more people are open to the practice. While this is certainly a good thing for everyone involved, it can be hard to discern hearsay from truth. Many marketers, for example, exploit the growing interest and lure those who do not know any better with products and false claims. Even though the benefits of meditation are steadily being verified by scientific inquiry, and celebrity testimonials enthrall the beginner's imagination, meditation does not promise immunity to life's ups and downs. Meditation is not a silver bullet or a magic pill. Unraveling your perceptions about meditation before you begin practicing will help to avert potential disappointments misinformation and the ego can create.

As with many new endeavors, various letdowns can undermine the best of intentions. Meditation, a lifelong endeavor, is fraught with misconceptions that can take the momentum out of the most enthusiastic meditator's sails. They can interfere at the beginning or even after twenty years of practice. Here are a few precautions to consider at the start, which experienced meditators would do well to remember and take to heart.

1. Children often quit playing a sport when they lose or for some reason decide they are not good enough. Notwithstanding all the coaches who preach the imperative of winning, as soon as things get hard, many of us tend to quit. Some people stop playing music when their public performance causes them embarrassment. Many of us have not been counseled on how to cope with failure. Unrealistic standards of perfection are the real impediments to success.

2. After a bad breakup, some folks are terrified of dating again. Misled by fairytales of romance, they were not fully aware of the risks intimacy entails. A realistic awareness of the potential gains and losses when we open ourselves would dispel the fantasies and seed resilience.

These scenarios are examples of one of the most difficult human feats: sustaining the focus of our consciousness for a prolonged period of time, especially when the going gets tough. This is also the difficulty we face with meditation. As with many things, we hear more about the glory and romance of meditation than we do its challenges. In popular discussions and even in the scientific reports, meditation's effects on reducing stress, improving energy, deepening relationships, and boosting creativity are emphasized. But focusing only on such benefits sets us up with high expectations from which we can crash if things do not go quite as planned. Meditation can be difficult—it requires tremendous discipline in the face of distractions of all kinds as well as the difficulties mental and emotional clarity can bring. When do we hear about the numbers of people who fall out of their good intention to meditate every day?

Knowledge of meditation's double-edged sword helps to prepare the mind and keep it open to whatever comes from the practice. This chapter explores some scenarios based on commonly held misconceptions about meditation. I encourage you to use them to become aware of your own expectations, assumptions, and misconceptions as you begin your meditation journey. Your awareness will empower you along the way.

As stated, this manual intends to guide you on a journey of self-discovery. *The guide needs to know the way* (in this case the components for a solid meditation practice), *but a guide only shows the way.* As an instructor, I have learned over the years that when you define, choose, and create your own meditation practice, it is more likely to work for two important reasons. First, you have no one to resist. Second, only *you* really know what you need; it is my job simply to give you some tools to identify what you need. The path of following another's program has not worked well in my experience, but if you are someone who prefers to follow a larger program, read through this book and then choose the established program or group that suits your disposition.

Let us begin the personal discovery process with your journal.

1. Define meditation as you understand it in your own words.

    This definition may be edited later, for it can change; it may also stay the same. In either case, you will refer back to this definition throughout your work with this book.

2. What benefits do you expect to receive from your meditation practice? Be honest with yourself.

Of course, individual answers will vary, anywhere from "I want enlightenment" or "I want my pain (whether depression, anxiety, back pain and so forth) to go away" to "I want to live to be a hundred years old" or "I just want a few minutes of peace and quiet a day."

3. What has led you to develop an interest in meditation?

Common responses include: a desire to manage stress, enhance creativity, manage pain, improve focus, and lower blood pressure.

4. What meditation practices have you already tried?

It is fine to be a beginner and pass on this question, just as it is fine to record a long list of meditation practices.

Expectations and Meditation

Expectations can be disastrous in many areas. When we project what we think an outcome should be and later have to face the reality that the outcome was out of our control, we feel the sting of broken expectations. We wish to control reality to make it what we want it to be, but the only things that we can actually control are our actions and reactions to reality. Expectations set us up for failure when reality hits home—and reality often hits pretty hard! Acknowledging what you know but being open to what you do not is one step toward overcoming the delusions of our expectations. Please use the following examples to help you evaluate your own expectations of meditation.

I heard that meditation is good for healing.

After struggling with a health condition but finding no remedy from other sources, Melanie turned to meditation after reading an article about its healing effects. When a month passed and nothing changed, she felt let down once again. Meditation was no different than anything else Melanie had tried. She later learned from a psychotherapist that meditation is a piece of a larger lifestyle that would improve her health—a lifestyle to be maintained in sickness and health.

Lesson: Make an inner spiritual principle the goal and let any physical effect be a welcome byproduct. A clearer mind does give us a greater awareness of our body's condition and a compassionate relationship to it, but be careful not to add pressure to your meditation practice to fix a health issue.

Meditation will reduce my chronic pain.

After trying just about everything else to alleviate repeated bouts of back pain, Jane decided she would meditate after learning from books on meditation that it could diminish pain. But Jane soon discovered that meditation was more difficult than she had expected and that sitting for long periods of time actually hurt her back. She was more than a little let down. How could she hope to do this beneficial practice if she was not physically able to sit comfortably? Fortunately, Jane subsequently learned that slow walking meditation, deep breathing, and relaxation exercises provide similar effects to sitting on a cushion. Lucky for Jane, she was resourceful enough to continue exploring when her original expectation was not met.

Lesson: Relaxation of the mind–body complex decreases the tension on nerves that often decreases pain as well. The expansion of consciousness, however, will also help us to accept pain with a new perspective, which also changes our experience of it.

I hope to have better relationships when I am calm and composed.

Despite his hope, Carl's meditation practice alone did not improve his marriage. It improved Carl's stress quotient, but his wife still had the same complaints. During a marital counseling session, Carl realized that he was not really listening to his wife; he was listening to his thoughts, not hers. When his mind and heart opened to her feelings, his marriage was saved. Meditation helped Carl to become more aware, which allowed him to see beyond himself and listen to another's point of view.

   Lesson: A still mind adapts better because its awareness is expanded.

A friend who meditates does not struggle with stress; my stress will vanish if I meditate too.

Throughout the years, Sally admired Joan, her genuinely calm and positive neighbor. Eventually, Sally joined Joan at her weekly meditation classes, and in time, Sally learned from Joan that she frequently sees a counselor and regularly studies literature about cultivating peace. Joan also exercises daily and eats a healthy diet. Sally realized that if she wanted the equanimity she admired in Joan, she too would have to do more than meditate.

   Lesson: Meditation is one tool for stress management among many that together create a lifestyle of well-being.

Meditation will help me double my salary because my creativity will be enhanced.

John is a workaholic who knows that overwork leads to diminishing returns. He chose to meditate in hopes of maximizing his productivity. His unemployed buddy Bill also meditates, believing it will manifest a job for him. Both men are meditating because they have misunderstood the popularized law of attraction: Focus on what you want, and you will attract it into your life. But John and Bill have not examined the essence of what they want. On the surface, both wanted better careers and financial gains, but deeper reflection enabled them to see that what they wanted was a happy, peaceful, and safe existence for their families. In time, Jon and Bill let go of their desire for material measures of success and instead started to cultivate their internal experience of success. They simplified their lives and used their money more consciously.

   Lesson: A stable mind can see what the real problems and solutions are, and what is truly needed or desired.

Meditation will answer my questions whenever I want it to.

Greg was at a standstill: Should he accept a promotion that would force him to move his family to another country, or should he pass on the promotion and keep his family rooted where they were? The family listed the pros and cons, but they were surprisingly equal. No one could see into the future, so Greg decided to find the answer by meditating on the question. But his meditations were full of disrupting thoughts; his ego persisted in its attempts to solve the situation. Finally, one day he let go of the ego's drive and stopped searching. A few weeks later, Greg shared this insight with his family: "Our happiness as a family will have to be found within each one of us. We can be happy here, and we can be happy in South America." The family finally decided to move because they thought the relocation would be fun and realized they could always return to their hometown in the future.

Lesson: When answers to questions are not clear, allow the answers to find you in their own time. They will find you when you are open enough to receive them.

I have been meditating for a few months, but nothing is happening.

After a few months in the meditation training class, Betty told her teacher that nothing was happening in her practice. Betty reported that she meditated every day at the same time, using the same technique, but months had passed and she still had not seen a light or heard an inner voice—the kinds of things she had read about in some of her New Age books. Betty's meditation instructor reminded her of what many of the meditation teachers throughout the ages had said about becoming distracted from the true Self by extrasensory phenomena. She also directed Betty to explore her experience and interpretation of "nothing."

Lesson: It is helpful to have a meditation mentor to consult with because it is tough to measure progress in meditation during meditation.

I thought meditation would decrease my thoughts, but they have increased!

At the last Introduction to Meditation class, Ralph announced to the group that he had regressed during the course. Instead of a calm mind, he found he was having more thoughts now than when he had started the course. Although he did not say it aloud, he wondered if he could get his money back. But then the teacher surprised him by announcing to the class, "Ralph has, in fact, successfully begun the meditation self-discovery process. If anyone else has also discovered that he or she has more thoughts now than at the beginning, know that it means your consciousness has risen above the thinking mind. In order to realize that your mind has a lot of thoughts, you must have arrived at a place from which you can observe your own mind. When you come to understand the roots of your thoughts, they will begin to subside. Great work, Ralph!"

Lesson: We see much turbulence when we are seated in the eye of the storm.

Assumptions and Meditation

If expectations are the fruit of an ego driven by knowledge, then assumptions are the fruit of an ego driven by incomplete understanding. A friend may constantly talk to you about his or her meditation classes, but hearing about meditation and actually practicing are quite different. It is easy to see how someone could fabricate hopes about what meditation will do based only on what he or she has heard about the practice. Hope, however, is often not grounded in truth. Hope can also rob us of the living moment as we anticipate "better" times in the future—times that may or may not manifest. To overcome assumptions, remember that knowledge is power against misguided hopes. The following scenarios will help you evaluate what you actually know and what you think you know about meditation practice.

I hear meditation is hard, so I am not interested in trying.

At various times in his life, Joe had tried meditation but to no avail. He believed it did not work for him, and if anything, he often found it uncomfortable. But when Joe learned a physical relaxation method, he started to experience more peace almost instantly, and when he learned a deep-breathing exercise, that sent him to a new level altogether. Once he also learned how to work with his thoughts to shift them in positive directions, he suddenly found that he could meditate.

Lesson: Learning the basics of meditation leads to a true experience of meditation and the gradual realization of its benefits.

*I am not the right type for
meditation because I am way too active.*

Connie was introduced to visualization by her neighbor and good friend. Listening to the tapes she was given and trying the practices, Connie could honestly say she saw nothing, though she did enjoy the opportunity to relax. When she later learned that there are six major methods of meditation, she found that mindfulness practices helped her to center and mantra practices came easily to her because she already knew the technique from prayers she had recited as a child.

Lesson: Finding your meditation type enhances your practice.

*Meditation takes too much time,
and life is too short to take that time.*

Between the demands of work, BlackBerrys, iPhones, laptops, texting, tweeting, and Facebooking, between shuttling the kids around and preparing meals and cleaning up, who has time for meditating? That time should be spent with the family, should it not? This is all true, however taking some quiet time when we wake or before we go to bed actually deepens our awareness and appreciation of all the little events that make up the day, instead of moving through the day in a constant blur and then crashing at the end of it.

Lesson: Meditation takes only twenty to thirty minutes a day, and the benefits enrich our lives with a more conscious and whole approach to living.

Meditation is an Eastern religion, and I am not interested in another religion.

Since childhood, Paul has been an active member in his church. He feels conflicted about meditation because his church does not recommend it but his girlfriend meditates daily. When Paul accompanies his girlfriend at her meditation center, he discovers that he enjoys it. Some of the books he has read on meditation preach a guru devotion or deity worship that is at odds with his religious convictions. Recently, he attended a meditation group that takes a more scientific approach and welcomes members from all religious faiths.

Lesson: Although there are meditation groups that blend their meditation practice with their dogmas, many meditation groups and practices are open to people of all faiths. Meditation practice can also be found in most religious traditions.

I just cannot be comfortable sitting on a tiny meditation cushion.

Simpson was a football lineman in college. With bad knees from numerous injuries and a muscular frame, he found sitting on a little meditation cushion intolerable, but he did want to quiet his mind. Simpson quit meditation because his knees just could not handle sitting on the cushion. When he later attended a meditation program in which the instructor permitted sitting in chairs, Simpson discovered that chairs were a comfortable and accessible method; he has not missed a day in his meditation chair.

Lesson: The most important aspect of the seated meditation position is that the spine is erect to maintain alertness. Sitting in a chair is perfectly acceptable.

I can learn meditation on my own.

Pete said he did not want to join a meditation class because he could learn it on his own. He had learned to build a car engine by taking an old car apart and then putting it back together, so why would he not be able to take his mind apart in meditation and put it back together again without help? After reading a few books on meditation and trying some of the methods off and on for a few years, Pete discovered he was not learning much from this approach. In the end, he found it much easier to build cars on his own than to understand the workings of his psyche on his own. After years as a "lone-ranger" meditator, Pete joined a class.

Lesson: Meditation requires guidance and community support to foster clear understanding and to maintain discipline.

I thought finding time for meditation would not be that hard.

Joe and Jean started practicing meditation together as a couple. As time went on and Joe's job changed, their schedules could not be easily coordinated. Except for an occasional class, the hectic work routine caused their meditation practice to fall by the wayside. Once again, business in the modern world proved to be the toughest hurdle to a meditation practice.

Lesson: Scheduling quiet time needs to be an active commitment in the face of modern society's obligations and stress.

Misconceptions and Meditation

Misconceptions are based either on partial or complete information that is misinterpreted or misconstrued. Misconceptions actually provide us with an opportunity for growth. Whatever misconceptions we may have, if we have an open mind and value learning, correcting misconceptions becomes a positive experience. However, those who feel that they must hold firmly to their opinions will experience letdowns when reality crashes through their misconceptions. Becoming aware of why we believe what we do—is it based on fact, experience, assumption and so forth—is primary to uncovering the truth. The following examples highlight some common misconceptions about meditation. Use these to evaluate your own ideas about meditation.

Meditation is only for people who are not active.

Bill is the kind of person who likes to get things done. He is an active fellow, who is disciplined about his exercise routine, diet, and overall lifestyle. Bill's discipline has helped him to overcome negative thinking and to become a model employee and leader at his company. However, he struggles with sleep because of the many ideas running around in his head. His mind just will not cooperate, unlike the disciplined control Bill is used to in other areas of his life. After a bout with self-schooled meditation, Bill decided it was for passive people, not active types like him, so he returned to physical exercise to cope with his busy mind. When his doctor recommended sleep medication, Bill was reluctant and continued his research, which suggested once again that meditation could help. This time around, Bill attended a course and discovered that meditation incorporates more than sitting still. He learned deep breathing and relaxation exercises, which helped with his sleep issues. He also learned to work with his thoughts through journaling. When almost a year had passed, Bill realized he was just scratching the surface of his mind's inner workings.

  Lesson: Sitting still externally does not mean we are not actively accomplishing much internally.

I am way too busy to meditate.

It was January, and Deborah's new year's resolution had her join her fifth meditation class, though she never completed the previous courses she had taken in the last few years. After the second night, Deborah realized that it was not her motivation or interest in meditation that kept her from completing the courses but her interest in so many other activities that distracted her. She volunteered weekly at the SPCA and a soup kitchen Saturday mornings, taught Sunday school, and visited her 98-year-old grandmother every week, in addition to caring for her two soccer-playing, music-loving kids. When she failed to complete her fifth meditation course, Deborah consulted with a yoga therapist. After deep reflection, she chose to stop volunteering while her kids were young, and her yoga therapist helped her set a new schedule for herself. Deborah now attends her sixth meditation course regularly and has even begun a midweek meditation group at her place of worship.

Lesson: It is true that if you are too busy, you cannot find time to meditate. Schedule your meditation time the way you would any other important event.

I can't meditate because I am an athletic, fitness-minded person. Meditation is too static a practice.

Triathlete and "super-mom" Elisa was a high-energy woman until an injury landed her in yoga and swimming classes. Both activities gave Elisa more time to reflect, especially the quiet time in yoga. She began to learn how to relax muscles that did not have to be engaged in different movements, and she began to learn rhythmic deep breathing. She applied what she was learning in yoga to swimming and found her stamina increased for the first time since her college days. Elisa discovered the value of keeping the mind focused for longer and longer durations of time.

Lesson: Even the strong of body have to train their minds.

If I want to meditate, I will have to join a monastery.

Susan woke up one day tired after a late night of partying. The party was fun, but Susan was in transition because she had begun studying meditation. She soon curtailed her drinking. She began staying home on the weekends except for her meditation class, family gatherings, and other outdoor activities. Susan read some very serious books that she did not realize were a bit outside what was normal for her. She started to isolate herself because she thought that the monastic way was the only way. Her extreme approach left her lonely. She tried to interest her friends in meditation but they never committed as she had. She created an all-or-nothing approach. Finally, her meditation teacher noticed her speaking in absolute statements about how meditation must be taken seriously. This broad-minded teacher helped Susan recognize that loving relationships with old friends and family is a key part of maintaining a balanced state of mind. As soon as Susan accepted that not everyone has to meditate to be happy, she relaxed and progressed.

Lesson: It is okay to make new friends who share your interest in meditation, and it is okay to have a variety of friends who reflect your different qualities and interests.

Meditation will heal my depression, so I will be able to stop taking medication for it.

Like many college students, Liam was still taking medication for anxiety and depression prescribed to him in high school. His reading led him to discover that meditation would balance his mind so he could stop taking medication. But his attempts to do this on his own threw him off balance. When he began working with a psychotherapist who taught meditation and yoga, Liam was able to decrease his dose and dependence on medication. He could not be sure though of what did the trick—meditation, therapy, or the stress management, relaxation, and breathing tools he learned—or a combination of them all.

Lesson: Meditation is indeed healing, but one method alone does not guarantee healing.

If I take meditation seriously, my emotions will cease.

Harold changed from an outgoing guy to a taciturn fellow, speaking only when necessary. He was applying the lessons his guru taught him and mastering his emotions. Harold took to heart the comments about the importance of emotional stability. This led Harold to treat the ups and downs of life as if he were meditating; he became very bland. However, Harold used to be a humorous guy. Eventually, his friends snapped him out of his seriousness and he gave up meditation because his friends were right, Harold had to be Harold. A year later, Harold returned to visit his guru with a question about how can he be himself as well as a meditator. His guru responded by laughing and joking with Harold. He told Harold to try a few joyful meditation exercises and recast his view of silence as austerity to silence as blissful.

Lesson: Maintain a balanced perspective. Do not forgo common sense, community support, or your natural disposition—not even for a kindhearted and well-intentioned guru.

No one told me I would face painful, repressed memories while meditating.

Jenny started meditation with the idea that it would deepen her sense of peace and bring all the positive effects she had read about into her life. She was an upbeat, high-energy person who made everyone around her feel good. At the same time, a close friend continually confronted Jenny with negativity and criticism, which she subconsciously internalized. After a few months of meditation practice, Jenny became more quiet and subdued. While she was still kind to everyone, she was not as exuberant. After a few more months of meditation, Jenny realized that if she was honest with herself, she could see that no matter how kind she was, not everyone can reciprocate—in particular, that close but fault-finding friend. Her friend may not have changed, but Jenny had. She learned to accept this person without internalizing the friend's negativity.

Lesson: A quiet mind purifies itself in self-awareness. Unresolved issues may be painful to confront, but peace and liberation occur when the mind is free of charged emotions and situations.

*I thought it would be easy to just start
meditating, but I can not seem to get into a routine.*

Like Bill and Deborah earlier who thought meditation would be easy, Jack found that when he sits down to meditate, despite his good intentions, he either falls asleep or becomes frustrated. After discussing this with a meditation mentor, Jack learned that he was trying the wrong exercises for his needs. Jack was using an advanced book on meditation, but he had not yet learned deep breathing, relaxation, or positive thinking. Once he was given the appropriate exercises, Jack's meditation experience was much more successful—he now looks forward to his quiet time.

Lesson: Learning to meditate involves numerous steps that can be applied gradually. Take it one step at a time. Pay careful attention to part II of this book.

Having read the various examples of expectations, assumptions, and misconceptions associated with meditation, now revisit your answers to the questions at the beginning of this chapter.

1. Define meditation as you understand it in your own words.
   Notice if your definition has changed or expanded.

2. What benefits do you expect to receive from your meditation practice?
   This time take any overblown and unrealistic responses you may have originally had and see how you can revise them to be more realistic. Instead of meditation curing your cancer, how about using meditation to minimize the stress you experience so that you can better cope with the situation?

3. What has led you to develop an interest in meditation?

4. Discuss how your interest finds its roots in a deeper need or needs.

Summary

1. Meditation involves an entire approach to life. It means both sitting quietly to focus the mind *and* approaching daily life with grace.

2. Meditation helps us cope with life's difficulties but does not solve them.

3. Meditation is a lifelong journey of self-discovery. We neither succeed nor fail when meditating; we observe what we may call success or failure.

4. Meditation is about your journey of self-discovery. You do not force-fit a meditation program into your life. You slowly align your life and a meditation practice using all the elements that comprise a meditation lifestyle.

5. Although it will challenge your mind, meditation should be comfortable for your body.

6. Because distractions are being eliminated, your mind may appear to have more thoughts than when you started meditating. As you come to understand these thoughts, self-discovery will continue to occur.

Two

....

How Your Past Informs Your Meditation Style

A literal definition of seated meditation is to sit and focus the mind on one object. The word "object" is intentionally vague because the object of focus depends on the method of meditation. Most methods are a variation of the one-thought focus. Some schools of meditation speak of having "no thoughts" during the practice, while others say that even no thought is a thought. Some schools of meditation emphasize mindfulness, and others emphasize not taking thought too seriously.

All these variations imply sitting quietly with your eyes closed. I want to expand the definition of meditation and use this book to introduce meditation as a process that unfolds in stages. The first stage involves self-inquiry in terms of recognizing your disposition, particularly your strengths, as well as your motivation. The next stage highlights the importance of a lifestyle conducive to sustained meditation practice, which part II covers. In part III, methods of meditation are explored so that you can discover a style that suits you. This manual then examines the subsequent stage, when the mind struggles by indulging in various resistances to prolonged practice.

My understanding of meditation applies the process of focusing the mind both during formal practice and throughout the day. This is an important lesson, which I will frequently state throughout the book: *meditation includes an entire approach to life.* After all, how can the same mind that was yelling uncontrollably an hour ago be expected to focus once the eyes are closed in seated meditation? Some people start working on their lives first and then proceed to seated meditation. Others start meditating and soon realize how important it is to quiet their reactions in daily affairs. Seated meditation exercises are one way to practice, but chopping vegetables and driving to work are also opportunities to practice.

Because the lifestyle choices you make to support your practice and the choices you make about the method of formal meditation you'll practice depend on such a diverse array of factors, my role is to guide you to create your individualized program. Plenty of programs already exist—in the form of DVDs, CDs, and expensive courses—that promise everything you could want from meditation. These programs may make tons of money for their producers, but they likely would prove to be an unsuccessful experience for you. I am interested in helping you by sharing information and tools that will enable you to make decisions that suit you. I encourage you to join a local meditation group once you determine which practice is best for you, but first I want you to learn by exploring what is best for you.

Throughout the stages in this process, changes will occur in your life. The program needs to be created by you so that you can mold it around your life. In a month or two, when something new occurs in your life, your program may need to be revised. You may move, change your job, or initiate some other major change, or it may be that a simple change in season requires the time of your daily walk to be revised. All of these changes, major and minor, will require you to adapt your meditation practice. Because of these unpredictable variables, there is no one way for everyone. What does work is when you, equipped with information and tools, take control of your personal meditation program.

There are a variety of psychological tests to classify personality types. You might be a Type A, a Myers-Briggs Intuitive, or an Ayurvedic *Vata*—but no matter how your personality type is categorized, you are unique. I find psychological tests fascinating—earning a doctorate in holistic healing, I have used many of these tests—but when I teach meditation I do not use them. I find that having students reflect and journal is an effective tool for self-understanding.

To continue with the journaling work, I would like you to reflect on at least five pivotal life experiences that left you with a quiet mind. Many people report on experiences as familiar yet remarkable as walking the dog, washing the dishes, cleaning the house, folding laundry, gardening, painting, singing, swimming, reading, and even riding a train. The collective list can be endless. You will return to your responses at the end of this chapter. And throughout the work we undertake together in this book, remember to enjoy the process. The journey is as important as the destination.

Phase 1

List activities from your past that have fostered a quiet mind. You can go as far back as childhood.

- What games or activities have quieted your mind?
- Do any religious experiences come to mind?
- Do any experiences in nature stand out?
- Do you have any previous experiences with meditation to report?
- Have you engaged in any hobbies that are relaxing?
- Are there occasions with pets or friends that had a relaxing effect?

• Have you used alcohol or other mood- or mind-altering substances that calmed you?

Be honest with yourself; these responses are for you as you explore your experiences with a peaceful state of mind and lay the foundation for a meditation program that suits you.

Our childhood experiences show us an unadulterated expression of our personality. Children have the almost limitless option of playing, and they play in ways that express their personality. Taking some time to recollect the activities that brought you peace at an early age will help you connect those foundational moments to the activities you pursued as you grew up. Your innate tendencies reflect your inherent strengths for meditation. This self-reflection will also be valuable in identifying what lifestyle areas need support. Since most adults lose the ample free-time of childhood, this exercise may be a refreshing reminder to practice some of those peaceful activities every now and again.

The exercises in this chapter help you begin to understand your own personality. As you work through the exercises below, reflect on the essence of the pivotal moments when you felt inner peace. Though it is not formal meditation, playing with the timeless abandon of a child can quiet the mind. Playing effortlessly can help create a mind that is receptive to meditation. Recall how you used to lose track of time. It might have been in nature, on occasions with close family or at religious gatherings. The important thing is to dwell on these positive moments so that you can understand what has helped you. The examples below are meant to help you deepen your understanding of what brought you peace in the past.

Phase 2

Analyze your childhood experiences of peace.

• Describe and title the experience.

• What was the feeling or emotion during this experience?

- Notice what you did and how you did it.

- Connect the aspects of this experience that brought
  your childhood mind peace.

EXAMPLE #1: BEDTIME PRAYER

One of the instructors at the YogaLife Institute says she used to line
up her stuffed animals on her pillow. Her precious animals took up so
much space that she almost fell out of bed! Despite the crowding, this
ritual gave her a great deal of inner peace and joy. This simple action of
affection reflects someone who finds peace of mind in ritual. Here are
her responses to the questions that conclude this chapter.

1. Describe and title the experience.

   Every night after my parents tucked me in, I lined up my stuffed
   animals on my bed. I pretended to fall asleep so my parents
   would leave the room, and then I tucked in my animals just as
   my parents had tucked me in. I am calling this experience "Bed-
   time Prayer."

2. What was the feeling or emotion during this experience?

   I felt a nurturing that brought contentment and peace to my heart
   because every one of my stuffed animals was happy and in its
   proper place.

3. Notice what you did and how you did it.

   I was very careful to line up all the animals, as though it were a
   religious ritual.

4. Connect the aspects of this experience that brought your
   childhood mind peace.

   I notice that arranging the animals lent me a sense of comfort.
   Today, as an adult, I observe how I like to place my spiritual journal to the left of my meditation candle and my spiritual readings

to the right, and I always light a candle during my practice. For a while I thought that this was superstitious, but now I can honor that what I recognize sets a good tone for my daily meditation practice.

Example #2: Zen Jogger

While he was growing up, a friend and yoga teacher said he was far from the athletic type, but the pressures of adolescence and the inspiration of some Olympic heroes spurred him to run track, where he also found peace of mind.

1. Describe and title the experience.

   Although not athletic by nature, I started jogging at age fifteen because I was tired of being the overweight kid. This was during the summer of the 1980 Olympics; the track stars inspired me with their fluid, almost effortless motion. I started running that summer and became the "Zen jogger."

2. What was the feeling or emotion during this experience?

   Initially, anger drove me to run, even though I could only make one lap around the block. After walking for a few minutes, my frustration with being out of shape propelled me to run another block. As I progressed, I began to feel invigorated, and eventually I gained self-esteem each time I extended the run. I realized that feeling tired was not the end, and I learned to run even when fatigued. In a few months, I was running to other neighborhoods, and my low self-esteem became a feeling of accomplishment. A year later, I became a member of a cross-country team.

3. Notice what you did and how you did it.

   When I ran, I started to find a rhythm with my feet, hands, and breath. I could hear each step as my running shoe gripped the pavement. The synchronization of breath, body, and sound mesmerized me though I was not conscious of it at the time. My mind felt empty of its usual self-conscious thoughts. The repetition seems to have been a good way for me to look within.

4. Connect the aspects of this experience that brought your childhood mind peace.

Having a goal is very important to me. I used to think that having a goal went against meditation, but now I see that a goal provides a positive direction. My goal gave me a purpose, which focused my energy in positive directions.

EXAMPLE #3: BOOKWORM

A meditation student purchased a small library of books on meditation. In fact, she has shelves of books—novels, travel books, cookbooks, and so forth. She loves reading, and if it were not for other responsibilities, she would read all night. As a child, she used a flashlight to read beneath her covers in bed while her parents thought she was soundly sleeping.

1. Describe and title the experience.

I liked to play outside with all the kids in the neighborhood. A game of tag and swimming at my friend's house were the most fun. But when it was time for games of sport, I preferred to read. When I was ten, I read *War and Peace,* and while some of it was beyond my comprehension, I used a dictionary to learn new words. All told, I was a serious bookworm.

2. What was the feeling or emotion during this experience?

Reading was a coping mechanism. It allowed me to relax, and helped me to use my imagination. I was also teaching myself more than I learned in school, where I was rather bored. Reading also shielded me from the moments of emotional instability in our house when my father was stressed.

3. Notice what you did and how you did it.

When I read, I was off by myself, which was rare for kids in my neighborhood. It set me apart in that way and also enabled me to speak with adults. I never thought of these things until now. Meditation is very similar to this.

4. Connect the aspects of this experience that brought your childhood mind peace.

Striving to go beyond my preconceived limits was a part of my personality—like the way I read *War and Peace* at ten. Learning definitely brings me a feeling of expansion and peace.

Summary

Look at your childhood experiences and use the questions below to help you analyze your personal approach to quieting your mind.

1. Describe and title the experience.

2. What was the feeling or emotion during this experience?

3. Notice what you did and how you did it.

4. Connect the aspects of this experience that brought your childhood mind peace.

Three

Your Daily Life and Meditation

Meditation equals stilling the mind. Because meditation is usually discussed as only sitting still in a contemplative pose, I will continue to remind you that every aspect of your life affects the mind's capacity for concentration and ease. This next building block in discovering your meditation type again requires that you be honest with yourself. Everything we do in our lives affects our mind, and everything we do also affects our karma, or future experiences.

While chapter 2 explored examples of peace from your past, this chapter examines the activities in your life at present. In the first set of exercises, you will list all the uplifting activities that presently give you a sense of peace. The second set of exercises examines activities that may offer temporary relief but ultimately move you away from a quiet mind. You will attempt to understand the roots of such activities in an effort to transform them. After all, the work of meditation is to transform the mind. Here we go!

A Doctor's Transformation

Being diagnosed with hypertension at forty brought Tom to yoga and meditation. Tom's family had a history of heart disease, and neither of his parents reached the age of sixty. Tom was a doctor and knew the benefits of healthy living; now he was ready to cultivate healthy habits himself. He knew that meditation was scientifically proven to lower blood pressure, and he wanted to learn. He signed up for a series of private lessons before joining any group classes.

To his surprise, instead of beginning with a bunch of directions, I asked Tom a simple question, "What relaxes you?" Though he was caught off guard, Tom answered easily that he enjoyed playing with his two golden retrievers. He walks the dogs every morning and evening without fail. Tom also noted that he loves gardening, but he could only do this on the weekends when the weather allowed. He had just lost fifteen pounds, but Tom did not rank going to the gym high on his enjoyment scale. However, he did enjoy the yoga classes he had begun to attend. He also liked reading self-help books and other educational reading, but because of the time his medical practice needed, he was not able to read as much as he might. Finally, Tom added that he loved having dinner with friends, his intimate relationship, and time visiting his extended family.

Step one of Tom's first assignment was partly completed. Now it is your turn. Write your responses in your journal.

Exercise 1: Uplifting Activities

1. List uplifting activities you presently enjoy.

   As a short aside, if you find activities like gambling relaxing, save that kind of activity for a forthcoming exercise. For now, take your time and list the more wholesome activities in your life. The list should be longer than you think. Here are some examples:

- going to the farmers' market
- chatting with neighbors
- reading the newspaper
- watching a favorite movie or TV show
- being out in nature
- taking walks
- listening to the radio
- playing with pet(s)
- hobbies

Even if you only find time to engage in a favorite activity seasonally or occasionally, include it. This list may also reflect some of the activities you enjoyed in your past (which you may have noted in the previous chapter's exercise).

2. Describe how you feel during each of the activities you listed.

   Tom caught me by surprise when he mentioned enjoying watering flowers. He explained how his garden brings him close to nature, which always evokes awe in him. He almost did not include this activity because he only has a small flower garden so the time spent doing this was easy to overlook. Be sure to include even small events like this one, and explain the feelings you experience with as much detail as you can.

3. Examine these positive feelings to uncover the underlying belief(s) connected to them.

   Tom began to uncover an underlying belief when he touched on the feeling of awe nature elicits in him. He continued to explain that feeling awe in nature expresses the gratitude he feels for his life. Life as a blessing is the core belief that inspired Tom to commit to medical school years ago.

You may find many answers as you touch upon your deeper beliefs and values, and some activities will evoke similar feelings and beliefs. For example, Tom found that playing with his dogs also connects him to gratitude for life. He believes a physician should practice what he preaches, so Tom keeps up with his exercise regimen. As you examine how an activity expresses a deep value or belief, also recognize how your values and beliefs have the power to calm your mind.

If you are feeling depressed or lost and cannot identify positive activities in your life right now, it would be wise to talk with a close friend or therapist for support.

4. How are the positive activities in my life connected to meditation?

This question directs you to see one of the major lessons in this book: our entire life is connected to meditation. Becoming more aware of the positive behaviors you already possess will enable you to discover ways to transform the daily tasks you find stressful. Your enjoyment of meditation and life overall will increase as your experience of stress decreases. These foundational exercises are important; return to them later whenever you feel stuck in your meditation practice.

As you identify your deeper beliefs, you will see that the first stages of meditation include understanding and effectively expressing your core beliefs throughout daily life.

Connie: A New Meditator

Connie, my mother, had her eye on our institute's programs from its start, but it took fourteen years for her to join a meditation class. One of the reasons she waited so long was that she felt a pressure to be a good student at her son's training center. When she did the exercises presented in this chapter though, her self-consciousness gave way to the delightful discovery that nearly everything in her life was already conducive to meditation. She just was not yet formally sitting in quiet. Here are some of the activities she listed, followed by the feelings and beliefs she uncovered.

Cooking healthy meals fills Connie's heart with love, and it allows her to express her belief in the power of nutrition to act as preventative medicine.

Walking her dog gives Connie a feeling of freedom. She is a nurturer by nature, and when she walks her dog, the walking invigorates her while she gets a sense of nurturing from her dog, Putter. She also likes the opportunity it gives her to visit with neighbors.

Bringing family together, babysitting grandchildren, and holidays bring comfort to Connie because she values tradition. Honoring family tradition also supports her belief that a loving family can go on to share their love with society at large.

Connie enjoys nature, which includes visiting the ocean, hiking, skiing, and playing golf. Being out in nature helps Connie to focus on the task at hand. Nothing else is in her mind when she walks in the woods or hits a golf ball. Honing her focus in nature relates to Connie's capacity to reach her full potential as she shifts into a zone of higher consciousness.

EXERCISE 2: LIMITING ACTIVITIES AND HABITS

In this next exercise, you will explore activities and habits that limit your well-being. As my mother observed in her development with meditation:

Meditation is more about understanding the patterns of your thinking that are ingrained. Meditation has helped me reprogram a few patterns I was unaware of, such as some of my reactions to other people and situations. Meditation helps you become keenly aware of your reactions, both positive and negative.

Tiffany's Oreo Blast Ice-Cream Meditation

One day in meditation class, Tiffany talked about her guilty pleasure: Oreo Blast ice cream. She smiled like a kid when she told the group about the bits of Oreo cookies that are mixed in with the vanilla ice cream. With summer's arrival, Tiffany told us she thinks about having ice cream after work throughout her day. Tiffany is a massage therapist, so she spends her day nurturing and healing others and the ice cream is her treat. Tiffany shared this habit in class as an example of a limiting habit that brings momentary happiness but negative consequences later. While most of us worry about gaining weight from ice cream, Tiffany's issue was feeling guilty. As a health professional, she knows that eating ice cream every night is not healthy. She feels hypocritical because she does not counsel her clients to eat ice cream after their massages but instead tells them to drink lemon water.

I asked the class to personify the activity that gives them temporary relief followed by negative effects. If the Oreo Blast could talk, Tiffany said it would say to her: "Honey, I am here just for you so that you can unwind and relax. You do not drink alcohol and you burn off a lot of calories at work, so just loosen up and have some fun." While she eats the ice cream, Tiffany feels like a kid and relaxes. Her burdens drop away, and she forgets her clients' concerns. But afterward, she says she feels "really, really guilty." This pattern of guilt continues to cycle around, and of course, in the end, guilt is not relaxing.

I also asked the class to identify the positive aspects of their guilty pleasure. Tiffany repeated the letting go of concerns and the shifting of gears at the end of the day. Her work can be tough when clients present difficult emotional issues and she is unable to help them. The Oreo Blast helps her reframe her perspective.

The transformational key for Tiffany was to figure out a guilt-free activity that would help her let go without compromising her health values. Tiffany loved the breathing aspects of her meditation practice, so for two weeks, she sat on the same couch on which she enjoyed the Oreo Blast and instead practiced ten minutes of undisturbed breathing exercises. She experience no guilt or internal resistance and felt empowered as she let go of the day's problems through breath-work. Such an immediate shift may not be everyone's experience, but Tiffany said her craving for ice cream just disappeared when she discovered what she really needed.

Now it is your turn to step up to the plate. Be brave, be honest, and free yourself.

1. List the activities you engage in to relax yourself but that actually set you back.

Many people use mind-altering substances such as alcohol, cigarettes, and even food. Some distract themselves with activities such as shopping or watching TV. Although such distractions may not be a full-blown addiction, their relief is temporary. It is important to be honest at this juncture. I have never seen anyone who did not have a few items for this list. Write down when and where you do this activity, how often and any other details that help you to examine your behavior. *Now continue by selecting one item from your list to work through in the rest of this exercise.* Please examine just one activity at a time.

2. Personify, or give a voice to, the activity.

Be creative at this stage and see what happens; you may be surprised. Allow the activity to speak to you, and again, be honest. If this exercise does not work for you, consider why you find yourself doing what you do. Try to name what you feel during the activity.

3. Distill the positive aspect of the activity.

How does it benefit you in a positive way? Tiffany was able to distill a feeling of "letting go" when she ate ice cream. What benefit(s) do you receive from your activity?

4. Identify the negative effects of the same activity.

Again, for Tiffany ice cream left her with guilty feelings, laced with sadness.

5. Use your knowledge of the benefits this activity provides to help you discover an activity that can give you the same benefits without unhealthy side effects.

Tiffany turned to deep breathing to let go, calm her mind, and oxygenate her body. Other options for relaxing might include taking a walk, cooking a healthy meal, or talking to a friend. Be careful not to force-fit an activity. You have to feel genuinely satisfied from the healthy activity you choose. This step also invites you to try out a new behavior to see if it actually uplifts you.

Added Help to Overcome Limiting Behaviors

When working with the pivotal step 3 in the exercise above, you may feel confused. It is not always easy to understand how drinking alcohol is supposed to be helpful, or you may become stuck on why you get lost in rerun episodes of your favorite TV show. You might find the chart below helpful as you determine which area of your life needs attention.

"Mind-body-spirit" is a popular idiom that captures a nonlinear way of thinking about ourselves. It relates the idea that our body, mind, and spirit affect one another. So, if the body is filled with wholesome foods that digest well, the mind and spirit are also positively affected. When the mind is given time to rest and the emotions time to settle, the body gains energy and the spirit thrives. Likewise, when the spirit is inspired by uplifting company or the study of scripture, the body and mind find peace as well. This paradigm can be expanded with two additional categories: energy and intellect. A philosophical construct found in the ancient Indian writings of the *Taittiriya Upanishad* holds that energy and intellect are attributes (named *koshas* in Sanskrit) that affect both the body and the mind.

Review the positive and negative summaries you wrote in the exercises above through the lens of these attributes: body, mind, spirit, energy, and intellect. When I teach students about nutrition, I use this paradigm and include more than just the physical food we eat. Tiffany's ice cream habit is a textbook case of attempting to feed emotions with food. When she gave herself time to breathe and consciously process her emotions instead, she felt more deeply satisfied. Use the chart below to see what aspect of yourself needs attention.

Body: The physical body needs food, rest, shelter, and hygiene.

Energy: Energy is created through exercise, breathing, and physical activity.

Mind: The "lower mind" relates to our emotions.

Intellect: The "higher mind" relates to ideas—as in thinking and studying.

Spirit: This is our belief system and includes religious thinking, prayer, and other activities that offer connection to a larger reality or higher power.

Here are some ways to use the chart above as you sort through addressing your true need(s) in a positive way.

Body: Limiting—I eat ice cream every night.
Positive—I take care to eat healthy foods in the right amounts.

Energy: Limiting—I push life to the limits and drink lots of caffeine to keep going.
Positive—I exercise daily and get to bed early for a good night's rest.

Mind: Limiting—I unwind by partying and venting with friends.
Positive—I talk with friends who help me understand life
events from a compassionate perspective.

Intellect: Limiting—I read anything to keep busy.
Positive—I read books that elevate my view of life's majesty
and mystery.

Spirit: Limiting—I attend church because it is what I am supposed
to do.
Positive—I stay involved with those who help me see the
bigger picture in life.

Summary

1. The exercises on identifying positive activities and behaviors in
your present life shed light on a variety of key points that will
inform the development of your meditation practice. Increase
the time you spend on such activities.

2. Limiting behaviors that are meant to be uplifting but offer
only temporary satisfaction need to be recognized so that they
can be transformed. The process of understanding these limiting
activities in order to transform them has begun.

3. All the exercises illustrate that meditation is not something
we do in addition to daily living but something that emanates
from all aspects of our lives and being.

Conclusion to Part I

Part I of this journey involved clarifying expectations, assumptions, and
misconceptions about meditation. This process helped you to understand your motivations and reframe them so that you will be prepared
to work on the self-transformation meditation fosters. In chapter 2, you
worked on understanding your natural disposition by recalling activities

from your past that brought you peace and well-being. In chapter 3, you returned to the present to recognize and honor activities and behaviors you presently engage in that support a meditative lifestyle of health and ease. Identifying those activities and behaviors that actually limit your well-being empowers you to reduce stress and improve mental focus in constructive ways that do not have negative side effects.

Part II
A New Lifestyle

After introducing meditation, its benefits, and some common misconceptions about practice, part II focuses on cultivating a meditative lifestyle. Meditation is much more than a daily allocation of time; unlike a regular exercise program meditation is not about "getting a workout in" for twenty to thirty minutes and then going back to the whirlwind of life. Instead, each of the next six chapters focuses on different aspects that are essential for transforming a short period of daily sitting meditation into a lifelong and continuous mindset. The goals of this particular section are threefold:

1. To help you minimize external stressors and internal stress responses as well as any activities that promote the "monkey mind." Just as it is difficult to see the bottom of a clear lake if the surface is rippled, it is nearly impossible to cultivate inner silence when the mind is disturbed by things without and within. Identifying the things that offset your natural inner peace can help foster awareness of your responses in the future.

2. To help you find or rediscover activities that suit your life which bring tranquility and peace of mind.

   Though service to others is the epitome of a meditative life, if we do not tend to ourselves through simple activities and self-care, we can never hope to serve others. Deeper reflection on your personal meditation journeys from chapter 3 may reveal some new insights or reignite old loves.

3. To help you find at least twenty to thirty minutes of time out of the busy day for meditation practice.

   Admittedly, in an increasingly fast-paced and ever-active world, finding the time to meditate is not an easy task. Evaluating your responsibilities and priorities (to others as well as yourself) can assist in finding those precious moments of silence.

Four
....

Identifying
Stressful Behaviors

I have often asked students new to meditation to tell me what they think are the "keys" to meditation. The usual responses might describe something related to a regular meditation exercise, proper deep breathing, or even just sitting quietly for a period of time each day. Most of us think that to meditate relates only to the time spent sitting still, but those few moments on the cushion or floor are only just the surface!

Coping with the "Monkey Mind"

For those who have been practicing meditation over the years, the effectiveness or success of meditation is better on some days than others, like anything else. Novice and veteran meditators have their days of mental disturbances as well as their days of stillness. The difference is that the beginner may attribute the meditative depth (or lack thereof) they achieve to have no particular cause. However, the amount of daily stress a person accrues and permits in the daily routine has a direct effect on that particular day's meditation session. What the veteran meditator is (usually) aware of is that the manner in which we live our lives greatly affects the waves on the lake of our minds. Entering a meditation session with a balanced mindset gives you a head start.

To begin to foster awareness of how your mind behaves, evaluate how much peace you experience in your daily life and routine. Hopefully there are moments of sanctuary: eating meals with the family, taking brief walks, during exercise. But what happens when you leave these environments? How does your mind react to waking up a bit late or to sitting in heavy traffic? Reflect on your relationships to an irascible boss or that coworker or client who gets on your last nerve. How do you handle situations when things do not quite go as you planned, at work or during other daily chores and activities? What about your relationships with those close to you: your family members, spouse or partner, children if you have them?

As you consider these elements of your life, please be honest but avoid being judgmental—the intent is awareness, not condemnation. If even one or two responses to just these examples were not even-keeled, most likely they will manifest when you sit down to meditate. The first step then is to be conscious of what upsets your inner peace and most importantly how you respond to these things. Remember, "stress" is nothing more than then the environment interacting with us, and it is constant. We cannot end the external stressors, but what we let in is entirely under our control.

Exercise 1: Listing Your Personal Stresses

As difficult as it may be, make a list of the things throughout your day that bring you stress. Do this with awareness and compassion. Try to capture every little detail from the moment you wake up until you drift off to sleep in the evening. Again, the intention is awareness; cultivate an objective and nonjudgmental attitude as best you can to get the most from this very informative exercise. No matter how long or short your list is, it is *your* list and will hopefully start to open you to patterns or behaviors you may not have been aware of at first. The intention of this exercise is to bring awareness at least once daily to one of the items on the list you have generated. Noticing your breathing as you sit in traffic or when someone cuts in front of you at the store; observing your emotions during and after a difficult conversation with a loved one or coworker; pausing for just a moment before responding to someone else's criticism—these are all very simple yet profound actions that can dramatically start to alter how your mind processes daily events.

From doing this exercise myself and with students, there are usually two types of items that appear on the lists. The more prevalent type is usually minor stresses; small irritations that can quickly accumulate throughout the course of a day or week. The awareness exercise above will hopefully assist you in sorting out these nuances from the other type of stresses on your list. It is my sincere hope that this second type, the greater stresses, are fewer in number. We all differ, but depending on our current life situations, some of these stresses may be quite encumbering and even detrimental. While awareness of these stresses is beneficial to begin learning to cope, in many cases a deeper reflection on their root cause is required to understand them on a foundational level.

EXERCISE 2: UNDERSTANDING THE ESSENCE OF STRESS

After cultivating compassionate awareness to some of the "little things" on your list, we will next choose two or three of the most stressful items for further introspection. It is quite possible that some of these items are very personal, so it is encouraged to perform these exercises in a private and comfortable setting for total honesty in your responses to the following questions. I find it helpful to jot each item atop a piece of scrap paper to give me plenty of room to freely explore this exercise. Fully and honestly work through each of the following questions. To get started, here are some examples of "big stressors" I have seen throughout the years:

- Overworked, too busy, rushed
- Technology overload
- Relationship difficulties (boss/coworkers or domestic/family)
- Constant worry
- Excessive behaviors (overeating, alcohol consumption, addictions)
- Insomnia or oversleeping

1. What time of day is your mind most disturbed and what particularly is it disturbed by?

2. How do you react and play into the disturbances created in your mind?

   For example, do you react to them impulsively, dwell on them for a time but keep silent, ignore them and let them sink into your subconscious, or some other response? Be as specific as you can.

3. What would you describe as the underlying attitude associated with these responses to the stressor?

   This point is most important and most avoided. You may have to physically feel the stressful sensation to understand it and give it a name. I am not advocating increasing your stress or to actively seek it as opposed to learning from it and moving towards transforming that feeling.

4. How do you feel in relationship **to** the stressor?

   For example, do you feel saddened, angered, frustrated, or anxious about it?

5. What is the corresponding psychological state fueling this feeling?

These include fear, egoism, attachment, aversion (dislike), or a faulty expectation.

Focus on the Opposite

With a statement of the psychological fuel for your responses to stress, we move towards a practice that can help shift the misalignment in the stressful situation toward a more peaceful balance. For each of the stressors you have chosen to analyze, contemplate and experiment with a virtue you feel would completely restore the balance in those situations. For example, many students mentioned struggling with speaking in public, even in small meditation group sessions. Nervousness, anxiety, and agitation were the most cited feelings and responses to the stressor, with fear being the primary psychological block. Courage can be a powerful opposing virtue which can then flow over into other aspects of your life. Acceptance or wisdom have also been helpful for others: accepting your self-criticism (for your audience may not criticize you at all!) and realizing that no speech nor audience will ever be "perfect."

Virtue in hand (and in mind), the exercise concludes by focusing on that concept and how you can practically apply the concept to the stressful situation. Your virtue (or virtues) becomes the positive point for centering and healing even amidst the former stressor. As the situation arises in the future and you find yourself responding to it, you may find it helpful to journal those responses and see how they change. Some may find it beneficial to return to this exercise, for as awareness grows so too may the underlying element of the stressor or the virtue needed to balance it.

Prioritizing and Time to Practice

Every so often when I am out in the woods on a hike or sitting on an empty beach, I find myself fantasizing about building a small hut and living off the land like our ancestors did for thousands of years. The quiet would be almost deafening; a quiet that we modern people pay hundreds of dollars and travel thousands of miles to attain at remote retreat centers—thinking that only in these far-off places will we find our true selves. Of course, I am forgetting about what would happen if there was a medical emergency or how I might start to crave intellectual discussions after a few months. During these quiet respites, I do remember to note a few ideas on how I can carve such moments of simplicity in everyday life.

There is no denying it, the modern world is moving at an alarming rate and worst of all we are accelerating. Computers are faster than they were even five years ago, and communication networks now expand across almost across every inch of our country, not to mention much of the globe. While even a few years ago most had cellular phones, now even children have portable Internet connections and just about everyone is connected to everyone else every moment of the day. While many technological advances have allowed for huge breakthroughs in the way of living, quality of life, and speed of information transfer, each new gadget only encourages and tempts the mind to also speed up. Recalling from part I, meditation is all about applying the brakes and slowing the mind down; it is an uphill battle against the modern world!

With that in mind, ask yourself how often you "unplug" from the world and go without electronic devices? And I mean *any* electronic device—no Internet, no television, no cell phone, or personal handheld. Your music player and even your watch are electronics too (unless you have an analog watch!). It is so easy to be connected to others for information and recreation that it is tempting to never pull the plug. But just like electronic devices, if you do not unplug *you* do not shut down, and thus is the fate of the modern mind. Stimuli from the natural environment become less of a factor considering the colossal amount of stimuli we are exposed to from the technology that is supposed to make our lives "simpler"; quite ironic!

Regarding recreation, how much of your previous "down time" do you find is occupied by technology? Use nonjudgment and objectivism in your response, but please be honest. How about your work life? Does your job require the ceaseless use of technology or is it a more traditional vocation? The pity of the modern paradigm is that the professions with simpler technology—and therefore less exposure to such stimuli—are looked upon with distaste in favor of the high tech and fast paced. If you have children or care for a child, consider their life in relation to technology and the activities they participate in—those that you have chosen as well as their inclinations.

As meditation aims to slow the mind down despite technology's urge to speed it up without rest, see if you can challenge yourself to "unplug" as fully as you can for a few hours one day in the coming week (in some cases we must have some connection due to the potential for emergencies, so this is not advocating complete aloofness!). Even if you can only get off of the grid for a few hours, be mindful of how you feel during and after the "getaway."

Shifting away from technology's role in recreation, take some time to examine other activities you engage in when not pursuing technology. Do you take time to read, and if so, what do you read? Though reading can help quiet the mind, depending on the content, some books can actually be more disturbing than television or the Internet. So while reading is definitely a break away from our web of technology, not all books are created equal. Nonfiction, philosophy, and spiritual texts tend to create the least mental waves and can provide further grounds for reflection and even focal points for meditation.

If you have children of your own or have close connections to children either through family or friends, examine how you interact, exercise, and play with them. Is it natural play and horsing around in sports or games, or is technology involved in some way? Do you find your-selves engaging the children in mental play with puzzles or tabletop games requiring thought and adeptness? Is the play a two-way street, where both you and the child take something away from it? A child's mind is much less disturbed by technology and stress (though in the rapid pace we live in, this is becoming frighteningly less so) and not only do they emulate and absorb our attitudes and actions in their pres-ence, but they also have much to teach us about simplicity, creative expression, and the joy of discovery.

For most of us, our jobs or schooling keep us indoors much of the day. When the work day is over and we move on to other chores or lei-sure time, how often do we find ourselves out in nature? From simply picking weeds in a garden or mowing the lawn to outdoor hikes and camping excursions, getting in touch with nature is perhaps the easiest way to slow down the mind. Nature moves at its own pace, and as any-one who has ever pined for the coming of spring or awaited the ripen-ing of a favorite fruit can attest, it is not usually very quick! In the midst of the natural, subdued pace the mind too begins to slow. In addition, the health benefits granted from being outdoors are more than worth it: fresh air, sunlight for vitamin D production and physical activity in any of a variety of forms. Barring weather of course, getting outside for even thirty minutes a day can be enough to reset the mental circuits back in tune with nature's rhythm.

Humans are social creatures—more and more noted by the success of social networking in the past few years—and this last section encour-ages you to critically evaluate your relationships to others at any level. From acquaintance to family member, examine the types of people that you interact with on a daily basis. Perhaps more than any other reflec-tion, it is imperative that you practice nonjudgment in this inquiry. The intention is not to criticize, condemn, or compare yourself to those in your life. Being social creatures, we play off of the feelings and actions of others. Those that have been a part of team sports know the sensation of feeling the victory of another's triumph, even if they were not in the game or the play themselves. Likewise, most humans still have some level of empathy remaining, and when someone is in despair, we feel for them. Bringing awareness to how our interactions with others have affected us can be eye-opening. Doing so shows us areas where perhaps we need to be less reactive or more open.

EXERCISE 3: EXAMINING YOUR PRIORITIES

Considering all the items discussed in this section, this last exercise hopes to facilitate a better understanding of your priorities as they are now. Things that rank lower on the list may be slowly substituted for activities that lend to a mindset more fruitful to meditation, depending on their importance. Begin by asking yourself: what is the most important thing to you in life? This "thing" need not even be a material thing. While all of life's facets are important, the perspective with which you hold priorities greatly affects your view of things. Which of your material pursuits most consume your time and energy? These pursuits may well be necessary as we all need food, shelter and clothing; but do we need gourmet food from high-class restaurants, two to three mortgages, and designer brand clothes?

1. Rank the following elements of the modern life in order from greatest to least priority where you are in your life right now.

   - Shelter

   - Finances

   - Food

   - Family time

   - Spiritual practice

   - Personal time

   - Recreation/Exercise

- Work

- Other personal category

Though you may wish for one of these to be a higher priority, do your best to honestly list them as they are.

2. Make (if you do not have one) or evaluate (if you do) your daily "To Do List."

Do you find that you are overactive, lazy, or pretty balanced in what activities you take on? If you are having trouble deciding, here is a hint: most people in modern culture need to choose to do less!

3. Once the "To Do List" is finished for the day (how often does that happen!), begin to note the activities you perform in the time that remains of the waking hours.

With whom do you interact; what sort of physical activity do you engage in? Do you have hobbies or special interests; are you active in the larger community?

With what you have to do and the priorities behind why you do it now in a little clearer focus, the task—for it will be a task—is to reflect on how important these activities really are. If you are one of many who do not believe they have the time to meditate, the journey to inner stillness begins with letting go of some activities that do not serve this purpose. In the beginning, meditation requires only ten to twenty minutes each day, so one option may be going to bed thirty minutes earlier so you can awaken just a bit earlier and meditate before you get ready for the day.

For those activities that are necessities like working and caring for children or family members, just because we are obliged to them does not mean that we cannot see them as empowering activities. Whenever you are working, be it at a job, around your home, or volunteering, con-centrating on the task at hand, no matter how small, can have dramatic effects on the mind. In the coming week, do your best to stay com-pletely focused on the task. You may find that as the mind fixes itself on a single point, the distractions and disturbances, though inevitable, have much less impact.

Five

········

Beyond Positive Thinking or Pure Thinking

If you have ever read some of the greatest meditation works, you are familiar with the fact that meditation teachings are often full of paradoxes. The classic book *Zen Mind, Beginner's Mind* by Suzuki Roshi names the most advanced meditator as one who can maintain a "beginner's mind." Distinguishing positive from pure thoughts is one such situation where defining meditation and the mind may sound unusual as positive and pure are very similar. A positive thought defines a situation in a good light, or with an uplifting description. A positive view of a rainy day could be, "Today's rain waters the flowers." A pure thought expression of a rainy day is different, "Today, it is raining." Notice how the pure thought just "is." The pure thought is very clear; no adjectives are needed, just bare fact. In normal life, it is OK to speak in positive ways and it is also fine to speak in pure ways. However, when meditating, the pure ways are more helpful because the pure "it just is" thinking lends to a completely quiet mind. Let us continue (another pure statement!).

The Story of the Stone Cutters

Once upon a time, a drought thrust an ancient kingdom into chaos. With the ground crusty and brittle, farmers could not tend the fields. Trouble started as some farmers took to gambling and others to theft. Fortunately, the king had enough grain stored to feed his people, and just as fortunately the king was very wise. The king declared that all unemployed farmers must begin work on a temple building project. In the hot sun, farmers started work at a quarry. The king's historian documented this exploit by interviewing the farmers-turned-stone-cutters. The men were crushing stone to build the foundation of the temple by swinging heavy mallets. The historian asked the first farmer what he was doing:

The first farmer said, "Can't you see? I am stuck in this hot sun because of this damn drought. I am forced like a slave to crack stone; cursed kingdom!"

The historian approached a clean-cut man who worked slowly and asked, "What are you doing?" The second farmer replied, "Yes, sir, to earn my food ration I am working eight hours a day cutting stone. We have water breaks and lunch is provided for us. I can support my family this way. Do I receive a bonus for sharing my views with you?"

Lastly, the historian went to another farmer and asked, "What are you doing?" This man continued cutting his stone until he reached a natural stopping point. He placed the mallet down, walked to the historian and said, "Can't you see, friend? I am building a temple."

The historian concluded that each farmer was outwardly cracking stone, yet their internal states of mind varied greatly. The first farmer's complaints of the working conditions were valid for all the farmers in that quarry: it was hot, dry, and dirty. The second, more self-centered farmer was also truthful in his comments that focused on doing the least amount of work for his pay.

In the Bhagavad Gita, a holy book that outlines yogic methods of stilling the mind, three qualities of reality are linked to the human beings state of mind. These first two farmers represent the negative and positive views respectively. It is taught that negative and positive are simply two sides of the same coin. The positive covers the negative by spinning reality from good to bad. The farmers agreed that they were in a bad situation: the first farmer shared the negative view, while the second farmer was making the best of a bad situation by looking at what he could gain from working in the quarry.

In terms of meditation, however, both of the first two men had very busy minds fraught with thoughts resisting reality. The negative man was stuck in the situation with no perspective and his emotions ran wild. The more contained "positive" fellow used a tremendous amount of creative energy to figure a way out of a situation that he disliked. Neither of these men can be blamed; it was a dire situation and they were coping.

Reading deeper into the Bhagavad Gita's qualities of reality, there is a third way of viewing life which is translated as "Pure." The third man was the only individual who was performing his work with a clear mind. He was not fighting the heat nor was he fantasizing about a future paycheck. He was enjoying the moment fully because he was able to view life on reality's terms. He saw the bigger picture. He appreciated the fact that the farmers were all building a new temple for their community. The "pure" perspective evokes a meditative mindset, completely embraces the good and bad in life without any resistance. This third farmer exemplifies the peace of mind that most every human being seeks and certainly that meditators aspire towards.

Twenty-five years of daily meditation has taught me to be less attached to life's daily ups and downs. Things like the weather and my friends' good or bad moods no longer disturb my mind as they once did. However, to say that suffering in the lives of my loved ones and the world at large does not bother me at times would be untrue. I care too deeply about others and as anyone on the spiritual path would say: to love is to feel and to feel can be painful at times. It is how I cope with the depth of our humanity that determines the level of my meditation. The exercises in the early part of this book that may surprise you or appear simplistic are important keys that you will revisit throughout your journey into the internal realms of your mind.

EXERCISE 1: CLASSIFYING STRESSORS

Return to the list of your life's stressors created in chapter 4, exercise 1. Place your typical coping methods to those stressors in one of the three categories:

1. Negative: Complaining, dwelling on the worst case, worry, depression, denial.

2. Positive: Seeing the bright side in spite of difficulty, dreaming of a better future.

3. Pure: Accepting life for what it is, and seeing deeper meaning in mundane activities.

EXAMPLE: HOMEWORK AS A YOUTH

1. Negative: As a child, I would often rather play outside and sometimes I would forget that I had homework. My forgetfulness was a form of denial. Other times, I would procrastinate and resist the homework in order to watch TV or talk to friends on the phone. These examples caused me to feel anxiety and not want to go to school on Monday morning.

2. Positive: As I reached high school and grades were going to determine my future, I studied because my future depended on it. Good grades equaled a successful future. Even though I did not like all the work, I pushed through it.

3. Pure: In certain subjects where the teacher applied the class to real life, I always got an "A." One biology teacher taught us how to make vinegar and wine, and demonstrated how and why earthquakes happen. He showed us how to clean cuts and why hydrogen peroxide kills germs. He was strict and inspiring all in one. We understood the bigger picture and all the kids were rapt in his classes.

Please write your responses to the stressors. When simple stressors are not resolved in the mind and transformed from the negative state to the pure state, the thoughts swirl in the meditator's mind. The added benefit is that your overall stress level decreases and your enjoyment of life, energy levels, and overall productivity increase!

Likes and Dislikes

Negative thoughts have a quality that I deem "sticky." The more intense the thought, the more it sticks in the mind and repeats. An annoying situation with a family member sticks in the mind and repeats over and over whereas an annoying fly is mild in intensity and once it buzzes by we quickly forget about it. One of the goals of meditation is to decrease the intensity of erroneous thoughts by learning to accept life and see things in the "pure" manner as mentioned above.

Major sources of these "sticky" thoughts are likes and dislikes. In meditation circles across many traditions likes and dislikes are considered related to human desires. Buddhism talks of desires; yoga talks of desires; and Western religions speak of appetites, sins, or impurity as the seat of a disturbed mind. No matter how you experience the roots of likes and dislikes, in meditation those value judgments create floods of uncontrollable thoughts.

Using our triad of positive, negative, and pure types of mindsets, likes represent positives and dislikes represent negatives. To define likes, they are things that are viewed as good, nice, and desired. Likes represent personality traits, as not all people like the same things—one person likes chocolate while another likes vanilla. Dislikes are the negatives to a person, unwanted things that are repelled. Negative and positive are described as polar opposites like north and south—both are still directions.

In terms of purity, likes and dislikes appear as self-created, self-serving illusions the mind uses to avoid a full connection to reality. A rainy day is wet; a sunny day is warmer. That type of food offers these nutritional values and tastes a certain way. "Purity" may appear devoid of passion, empty or downright boring on the surface, however the pure mind remains open, alive, and ever-experiencing. The pure mind can eat good food and stop when full and the pure mind can accept pain without suffering. Destructive events are witnessed from a broad viewpoint that is stable and healing. The following exercise will begin the journey of understating likes, dislikes, and reality.

Exercise 2: Drawing Your Likes and Dislikes

On a page, draw a rough outline of a human body (representing your life) with ample room inside of the body as well as outside the body. Place a circle around your body and within that circle write all the things in life that you like. Be detailed! List your favorite foods, friends, hobbies, books, memories, qualities about you, qualities about others, spiritual aspects of life, accomplishments, and anything that you like. Let this circle be filled with your likes.

Outside of this circle, write all of your dislikes, being just as detailed as with the first list. If you do not like weeds in your lawn, write it down. If you have a quarrel with a family member and you are on less than good terms right now, add it. Keep writing anything you dislike. Above all, be honest with yourself.

Now for the insight of the exercise: realize that everything on this page represents thoughts that you have on a regular basis. *These thoughts are you.* You are both what is inside and outside of the circle—all of it is you. What that means is that if you disliked a coworker, the qualities you disliked are being carried with you in your mind's aura. Those thoughts will show up when you try to meditate as well as any other similarly negatively charged situation that your mind interprets. Normally the mind thinks that dislike equals separation from an unwanted thing, person, or situation. However, dislike to a meditator is more like Super Glue; the thought sticks to the mind and repeats over and over.

Keep this paper and we will continue to understand these likes and dislikes. The goal in the following exercises is to de-stick, unclutter, and clear the mind of likes and dislikes.

Exercise 3: List Likes and Dislikes

List your predominant likes and dislikes in the categories similar to the examples below. Of course, feel free to add personal examples that may not be listed.

1. Foods: I like this tasty food, but I do not like that the same tasty food is fattening.

2. Spouse: I love my spouse's sense of humor, but I find my spouse's obsession with cleanliness disturbing.

3. Family: I love our reunions, I just find so-and-so's opinions troubling.

4. Work: I enjoy relating to customers but I do not like the staff meetings. I like one coworker, while I dislike another.

5. Hobby: I like bird watching, but I do not like how urban sprawl decreases bird habitats.

6. Myself: I like that I am disciplined, yet I do not like it that I am impatient.

Review the above list and rewrite the entries in terms of pure thoughts.

1. Foods: That tasty food's sugar content causes the body to store fat.

2. My spouse's humor stems from childhood tension. S/he had no control as a child, hence s/he finds a clean home to be reassuring and healing.

3. Reunions are filled with love and all families have opinionated members.

4. The work behind the scenes for serving customers is more difficult than caring for the customers.

5. Urban sprawl has been continuing since the industrial revolution. My love of bird watching is a way of reconnecting with nature in the midst of human progress.

6. I am disciplined and impatient, and like all people, I am learning acceptance.

   Begin to view your life in an open-minded fashion and observe how likes and dislikes interfere with your daily happiness. Work on seeing things with the pure mind and notice how your mind remains calmer during the day and calmer during meditation. The takeaway in terms of your meditation practice is that like a waterfall, thoughts keep tumbling in the mind even as one meditates. The pure mind is able to accept these thoughts but not think them. This is a skill that you may have developed in certain areas of your life where your concentration is very trained. Meditation elevates this skill to the level of being concentrated with a very subtle concentration point.

Eustress—The "Pure," or Good, Stress

Though it has been mentioned in this and previous chapters, it bears mentioning once again: stress is not necessarily always negative, it simply is! Stress is an environmental stimulus and in the right context can be a positive experience. Consider exercise: are not rigorous cardiovascular workouts or resistance training taxing on the body? Yes, however the benefits of regular exercise far outweigh not doing so. With the awareness cultivated in the reflection on those things that "stress" us above, we can now direct that same open, nonjudgmental mindfulness on the good kind of stress: eustress (*eu* is a Greek prefix meaning good or well).

EXERCISE 4: LISTING THE POSITIVE "EUSTRESS"

It may be helpful to go back to the personal meditation journey exercise from chapter 1. Useful gems of information about "eustressful" activities from your past may be found there. If some of those elements have carried through time into your current lifestyle, that's fantastic. If not, you may find it quite refreshing to retouch on those past loves. With the past in context, draw the awareness towards the present and to times when you are content, relaxed, and even peaceful during the day. Examples from earlier in the guide could be a leisurely breakfast, a solitary walk, or daily exercise that brings you nearer to stillness. The emphasis is more on the feeling from the activity, and not so much the object of the activity. Attaching peace to material objects is inherently flawed, something we'll discuss in later chapters.

Another "eustressful" activity is being helpful and showing kindness to others. Prolific spiritual author Ecknath Easwaran discusses "putting others first" (from his meditation program) as a fantastic exercise to move away from the self-centered, stress-inducing way of being towards a way of more joyful living by serving others. The modern movements of "random acts of kindness" and "paying it forward" are powerful ideas that honor benevolent acts. As you compile your list of peaceful times throughout your day, see if you can find places were you could insert a random act of kindness, and imagine how that might make your mind feel more serene.

EXERCISE 5: DAILY REFLECTION EXERCISE

Use any of these exercises on a daily basis if you feel drawn to them. Remember that there are hundreds of exercises and choose only the exercise that seems to offer you the most insight.

During the week, observe how your likes and dislikes affect your mind. Notice your reaction when you detect a like or a dislike emerging. During your ten minutes of daily reflection time, continue processing the likes and dislikes. Understand the roots of these thoughts. Next, attempt to develop a pure mode of viewing life.

For two minutes, review the previous day by examining events sequentially from morning to evening. Notice any events that were emotionally charged and reflect on that event to contain it in your mind. A good hint as to which events were emotionally charged: more than likely they are the ones you reflect on for more than a few moments.

For the next two minutes, see the following day from a "pure" perspective. If you are going to work, think of times when you can avoid a like/dislike confrontation and plan how you will remain pure instead. Think about your commute and be accepting of the traffic. Do this daily as a preventative measure.

Summary

During a six-month intensive residential study at the Yoga Institute in Mumbai, India in 1989, I resisted a line that was repeated in lectures for two months solid. The line was this: "Life is neutral. It is the mind that makes things stressful." The context of this teaching was not a blanket statement that stress does not exist; it was that most mundane chores or situations that we interpret as stressful are inherently neutral. Things like traffic are neutral; traffic is traffic. Most of us are in transit for the purpose of reaching our destination, and few folks plan to sit in traffic! However, it is true that my reaction to traffic determines the type of emotional life I lead. And, my emotional choices determine my stress level.

At the time in India while the traffic was really bad, my main challenge to this statement was an overbearing woman who decided she was going to be my stand-in "mother." I was twenty-five at the time and capable of determining how much to eat and how to handle various affairs of life. But in the midst of the serene yoga ashram, she pestered me at every lunchtime meal to eat more food. I thought there was no way this woman was neutral—more like neurotic!

After my months of study, I decided to test out this "pure thinking" theory one day and I just ignored her. I waited at lunch and when she walked over trying to force seconds on me, I thought, "tight on time, aren't you." In response, I accepted a few vegetables from her with no charged reaction. As soon as I did this, I noticed that she went around to the next fellow and that, in fact, she was pestering every man in the dining hall.

Inside I smiled and realized that if I did not react to her, she was really no disturbance. Later I learned that her children were all grown and that her husband had recently passed away. She had no one to nurture and was grieving in her own right. Her nurturing of us in the dining room was more important to her than I had understood previously.

Stressors are greatly affected by individual reactions. By understanding how your mind works, you can shift the effect of stressful situations. Keeping the mind less stressed greatly supports a meditation practice, brings peace of mind, and is good for your health.

Six

....

Deep Breathing

Breathing exercises were implemented in the field of yoga for thousands of years as an aid to calming the mind. *While in deep states of meditation, yogis realized that the breathing rate diminished.* As the yogi would wish to reenter the deep mental state, one of the first steps was to slow the breathing. Hence, when teaching meditation to students, the yogi began by showing students how to breathe deeply.

Once at a group meditation, I sat next to an older man (he was probably as old as I am now, but this was twenty years ago!). He was sitting on a church pew, slightly hunched. While he was not very large, in the slouched position his stomach expanded and blocked his diaphragm from moving. Consequently, his breathing was very rapid and shallow, meaning that only the upper respiratory cavity moved (clavicle breathing). In addition, he breathed very quickly—roughly one to two seconds in and one or two seconds out—overall his breath was quite forced and audible.

Breath and the Mind

"As the breath goes, so does the mind" says the yogic oral tradition. The difficulty with breathing so rapidly is that the nervous system, as well as every other system of the body, is largely regulated by the breathing patterns. Breathe in a rapid fashion as if you are stressed and your body will digest its food differently than if you breathe in a slow and deep fashion. The nervous system heightens when the breathing is shallow. You can play around with it on your own: breathe a few quick, shallow breaths and see if you can keep yourself from having an emotional reaction related to fear or anxiety!

As a younger graduate student at the time of observing this man, I was perplexed. He was a kind and deep-thinking person yet his breath did not match his mind. I had no way of sharing this information, yet I still remember the event: this is how important deep breathing is. I was unable to help him, as unsolicited breathing advice is just not an accepted cultural practice. However, you can use this example to learn and reap all the benefits of deep breathing.

The moral of this short story is that the thoughts in our mind, which are so difficult to stop or slow down, are regulated by breathing patterns. While this book glosses over the hundreds of proven health benefits of deep breathing, the quieting of the mind is greatly enhanced by some deep breathing. I cannot prove this assertion scientifically without a large research study, but it is plausible that most of the physiological benefits resulting from meditation are related to the fact that breathing slows while meditating.

Students new to deep breathing often feel as though they are meditating for the first few weeks when performing the slower deep breathing exercises. During this chapter, you are bound to slow down your thoughts and discover yet another key preparation for meditation, without which you would find it tough to quiet your mind.

A Few Key Reasons Why Deep Breathing Is So Effective for Meditation

Diaphragm (or belly) breathing is most important to include in your daily breathing because the majority of the lung's red blood cells are concentrated in the lowest areas of the lungs. This increases oxygen absorption that leads to increased vitality and an altered mind. Meditation requires alertness in spite of it looking easy. Secondly, as the belly is moved by the diaphragm in and out, blood circulates throughout the body and the heart relaxes. Try it: pull in the diaphragm as you exhale and expand the breath into the abdominal area for a few breaths and feel the circulatory effects.

While it may require time to maximize, breathing into the lateral area of the lungs by expanding the rib cage to the sides is just as important a part of a full breath. To be fully clear, this second facet of a deep breath is the sideways expansion of the lungs. The intercostals muscles, if not used on a regular basis, become stiff like any other muscle. As you open the lungs laterally, you further slow down the process of breathing. What may have been a quick two-second inhalation is immediately slowed by the diaphragm and intercostals movements. This slowing allows the small balloon-shaped air sacs, the alveoli, to fully expand and thereby promote greater oxygen absorption. On an emotional level, the slow breath tells the nervous system that you are in a stable, safe environment. Breathing is paramount to the health of mind and body.

As the air travels from the bottom of the lungs upward, the final area to expand is the clavicle or upper chest area. While most people do breathe into this upper region, it is usually just the very front of the upper chest where your hand would rest comfortably on your breast plate. However, if you expand the upper chest area slowly and continue until you feel the air flow into the very top of the lungs, you will notice that rarely does anyone fill that top area. It may feel refreshing and it will take at least two seconds to completely expand this final region of the lungs. Remember, the alveoli sacs resemble balloons and they need to be given time to fully inflate, just like a real balloon.

Exhaling offers a host of benefits as well. First of all, a proper exhalation allows there to be a more complete removal of carbon dioxide or "dead air" from the lungs and therefore the potential for a deep inhalation to follow. First, squeeze the upper chest followed by pulling in the ribcage and finally squeezing your stomach back toward the spine. Now, you are energized naturally!

After some time of regular practice for five minutes twice daily along with periodic breathing observations during the day, your breathing cycle will slowly become deeper automatically.

Breath, Mind, and Sanity— Your Sanity!

"In-Spirit-Action," or inspiration, means both the act of bringing air into the lungs and divine influence. The act of breathing is at once physical, biological, and tactile. The very act of breathing is our most vital of all lifelines; without breath, no creature would be alive. Breathing connects all living creatures with the environment. One way of summarizing human suffering is isolation from the larger universe. Meanwhile, breathing is absolute evidence that human beings are not only dependent upon nature for existence but that we are intimately connected to nature with every breath. So, to savor, honor, and revere breathing is akin to respecting the spiritual aspect of all beings.

The word "inspiration" is one of the key principles for meditation. In moments of silent reflection, the human being is able to step outside of the humdrum of anthropocentric thinking to step into a larger awareness that begets spiritual fulfillment, joy, and meaning.

Exercise 1: Breathing Self-Evaluation
It is important to know where you are when first learning an activity akin to deep breathing. If you are a long-term meditator and understand

your breathing pattern, please learn from this exercise as if you were a beginner observing breathing for the first time. Breathing alters with our stress level and our state of mind, and it is literally a lifelong life-line. Proper deep breathing is essentially the most important health choice we can actively make, as without breath for just four minutes, the human body ceases life-supporting function. Paradoxically, for all they instruct, schools do not teach proper deep breathing to young students.

To learn the effects of improper breathing on your physique and mind, sit in a slumping posture you know is a personal habit of yours. If you are unaware of a slouching position, imagine that you are sitting in front of a computer keyboard with your shoulders and upper body rounded and curved forward. Even though you know that this posture is incorrect, remain in the position and consider the questions to follow. This exercise is safe to use with children or friends, as you are only learning from observation. In fact, all of the breathing exercises below are intentionally simple and available to all fitness levels.

- What part of your lungs moves while you are in your slouched position? The areas to consider are the diaphragm (belly), ribcage, and upper chest (clavicle) regions.

- Which parts of the lungs are restricted in this posture? Consider the same areas as above.

- How many seconds do you inhale? How many seconds do you exhale? Is there a pause after inhalation, exhalation, or both?

- If you noticed a pause at any point, how long did it last? What is the quality of the breathing? Some examples are: choppy, in stages like an elevator, starts fast and slows, starts slow and increases. Be creative in describing your unique breath pattern—the goal is observation after all!

- How do you feel emotionally in this breath?

- To assist in emotional understanding, use your arms and hands to exaggerate the feeling associated with this breathing pattern and observe any accompanying facial expression(s).

- Keep your notes from these observations as we navigate through a series of exercises that will help to improve the quality of your breathing.

Posture Is First

Needless to say, during my first meditation experience in Japan, my legs felt as though they had fallen off of my body. Never had my legs been asleep for so long and never before had I sat on a *zafu* (a meditation cushion) let alone knowing that the cushion was called a zafu! Before even considering meditation, we must make sure that you know how to sit and why. In order to be successful with breathing, the spine needs to be erect and the arms and legs comfortable. No matter who you are, breathing begins with the physical positioning of the body. It is most important to keep in mind that if you feel any physical pain from sitting in meditation, you are instructed to reposition your body. Despite the common image of a monk sitting stone still for hours in meditation, such rigid positioning not only shuts off body awareness but can also be detrimental to the cushioning mechanisms of your bones and muscles. Do not worry if others are in the room with you, the noise created by you moving is of little to no interference to them. An injured knee, on the other hand, is a definite interference to your present and future practice.

Let this point be reiterated: **If you feel any physical pain from sitting in meditation, you are instructed to reposition your body.**

Key Principles

1. Lying down is not suitable for meditation: in spite of what people may say, lying down (supine position) is for relaxation.

In this position, sleep occurs for almost all people, even the most experienced meditator, within eight to twelve minutes.

2. Keep the spine erect and the core upright, as this allows maximum blood flow to the brain—therefore keeping you alert and aware in your practice. In addition, an erect spine permits proper breathing; even a slight lean forward can compress the lungs and diaphragm, reducing breathing capacity.

3. It has been shown that having a slight smile on your face can help facilitate a relaxation of the entire body. Such a "half-grin" also helps settle the shoulders and calm the mind.

4. Find a position that makes your legs as comfortable as possible. Remember that pain is to be avoided—sitting in a chair is permitted if necessary.

5. Be careful of your tailbone and coccyx. Improper sitting will compress the area at the base of the spine.

6. Keep your pelvis tilted slightly forward (but not the torso) to use the skeleton to support the upper body. When someone sits with a rounded low back due to a pelvis tilted backwards, the lower back will begin to ache shortly. Sitting in a chair is best if this happens to be the case.

7. While seated with the legs crossed in some fashion offers the idea of stillness and acceptance of one's situation, the legs may be placed in any comfortable position, really. Having the legs externally opened in a butterfly position or internally rotated in a kneeling position (with a blanket or bolster for support) are equally acceptable.

8. If you practice seated meditation, be sure to vary the posture so you won't strain the body by sitting in one position all the time.

9. If you opt for using a cushion, sit close to the front edge of it and let your crossed legs rest on the floor in front of you. Make sure that you never sit way back on the cushion, as this will cause the front edge to press the underside of the thigh, cutting off circulation, and leading to a lot of leg pain.

10. Be careful of the positioning and integrity of your knees in any seated posture. Be mindful of the position and compressive forces working on your lower back. Remember that you are always certainly permitted to meditate in a chair for better support and comfort.

Acceptable Poses for Meditation

The key principles above lead themselves into some of the most common postures well suited for meditation. Please keep in mind that one this is not an end-all list, and two it is more important to listen to your own body than follow someone's direct commands regarding a comfortable meditative posture. Comfort is predominantly subjective—so long as muscles and joints are not compromised—so use your own body's intuition to find what works best for you. As the body can become stilled, so too will follow the mind. Finding *your* meditation pose (or poses) is the first step.

Easy Pose—Simply sit cross-legged on the floor. Use a pillow or a blanket to keep the pelvis tilted forward if necessary. Be careful of the positioning of the legs so that they do not put undo pressure on your ankles or knees. Please be aware that while this pose is named "easy," you may find it to be quite challenging at first!

Lotus Pose—From easy pose, you next move your feet up into your lap. While this position is historically "the" meditation pose, be aware that it requires a good deal of flexibility as well as particular joint construction in the hips. If your hip joint anatomically cannot fully rotate externally, this position can be unreachable. For those who can physically get into the posture, it can cause great pressure on the knees. Be sure not to remain in this position beyond a few minutes, and alternate the front-facing shin.

Half-Lotus Pose—From the easy pose, instead of bringing both feet into the lap, only one foot is elevated. This tends to be easier than a full lotus position as less flexibility and extreme external rotation of the hip is required. Like the full lotus position, however, it is advisable not to remain in this posture for too long and to alternate which foot is placed in the lap.

Adamant Pose—From a kneeling position, fold the legs and sit the bottom down onto the heels of the feet, keeping both the knees and feet together. This position requires an intense fold of the legs, which can be impeded by tight quadriceps or ankles. This position can also put excessive strain on the knee joint, so you may wish to use a meditation bench, bolster, or blanket to help support the thighs. Traditionally, the tops of the feet rest on the ground but as mentioned above, this can be difficult on the ankles. The toes can be flexed so that the ball of the foot rests on the ground instead. This can be taxing on the toes, but also provides some elevation to ease the knees. With a support, this position can usually be held for a prolonged period of time, but without it is not recommended to hold for too long.

Butterfly Pose—From seated on the ground, bring the soles of the feet together and let the knees fall out and apart. Like the Lotus Pose above, the ease of even getting into this posture is dependent on the structure of the hip joint and flexibility in the groin. The knees may never reach the ground even in the most flexible individual if the hip joint does not allow for full external rotation. The use of folded blankets or blocks beneath each knee can help alleviate any holding in the legs. Unlike the other seated positions, it is very easy to round the low back sitting in this manner. The placement of a blanket beneath your bottom can help facilitate an easy tilt of the pelvis forward, thus relieving undo compression in the low back.

Sitting in a Chair—As cannot be stressed enough, sitting on the floor may just not be good for you, so you are always permitted to use a chair instead. When choosing a chair, ensure that it has a level seat, a straight back and no arms. It is best to situate yourself in such a way that your back does not lean against the chair's back. Also, it is very important that the front of the seat not dig into the underside of your thighs, as this can cut off circulation to your lower legs. Once situated on the chair seat, bring your legs together and place your feet flat on the floor to maintain a neutral pelvis.

Standing Prayer Pose—Believe it or not, you can meditate standing! There are inherent challenges with this position, namely falling over, so ensure that the area around you is safe and clear of items. Standing comfortably, bring the feet together or if your balance is weak, it is acceptable to place the feet a few inches apart. Bring your hands up to your heart with the palms together, letting the elbows relax. You are not so much pressing the hands strongly together (that would raise the elbows) as letting them rest on your chest so that the elbows are heavy with gravity. Keep your posture as upright as possible and slowly begin to close your eyes as you move towards quieting the mind.

Simple Breathing Exercises
for Meditation

In this section, you will learn a series of breathing exercises, of which only the last will be used as a preparation for even formal observance in meditation. The first three exercises are introduced to begin opening the lungs and for gaining awareness of your full respiratory potential. These exercises may be performed by anyone in any health condition, except of course any injury that could impede lung movement. Please note that the purpose of these exercises is simply to develop a slow inhalation and exhalation. The amount of time for the breath will vary; however, each area of the lungs will be in operation with practice and attention.

The exercises to follow, though listed sequentially, are not exercises to be "mastered" before moving on to the next. This is not to say that I do not recommend following them in the order they are listed, moving on to the exercises to follow only when you feel comfortable with the current breathing activity. Recall the concept of "beginner's mind"— each of these exercises is just as powerful to the regular practitioner as they are to the novice for the awareness that can be applied and continually cultivated.

EXERCISE 2: DIAPHRAGM BREATHING (PART 1 OF 3)

Breathing with the large diaphragm muscle in the center of your body is the first stage for the full yogic three-part deep breath. It is imperative to learn awareness and control of this essential muscle for the fullest potential of your breath is impossible without utilizing it. This type of breath is also recommended for emotional control—especially anger— because it gives you the time and space to become quiet, increasing internal awareness and emotional integration.

1. Lie comfortably on your back (supine position) and pull the knees up, placing the feet near your buttocks.

2. Place your right hand on your abdomen, and see if you can breathe only by moving the diaphragm up and down (your right hand should rise and fall with the breath).

3. Place your left hand on the upper chest area and see if you can keep the left hand from rising and falling as you continue to breathe. A neat fact: watch a baby sometime and you will see

that they breathe in this fashion naturally! It is only with age that we "forget" this completely normal breath pattern.

4. Keep the breath to a steady rhythm, starting with a three-second count in and a three-second count out. You may increase the count as comfortable to a maximum of ten seconds in and out.

5. Perform ten rounds (one inhale and exhale cycle is considered a round).

EXERCISE 3: INTERCOSTAL BREATHING (PART 2 OF 3)

Breathing laterally into the rib cage is perhaps the most difficult part of the breath to learn as it is quite challenging to isolate this region. In addition, the intercostal muscles that lie between the ribs are usually so unused that they tend to "lock" and further prevent conscious control. Using the following exercise, however, freedom of motion can be achieved. To begin to cultivate awareness of this region, we start with a simple preparatory exercise.

1. Sit comfortably on the floor or in a chair, and lean forward with the torso ever so slightly.

2. Carefully arch the midback to engage the intercostals for support and opening of the lungs. As you breathe, be careful to avoid breathing into the upper lungs, as this actually restricts lateral movement.

As you learn to notice these muscles, you can proceed to the formal exercise.

1. Sit or stand erect with your feet shoulder-width apart.

2. Place your hands on the lower portion of the rib cage, just below the chest.

3. As you inhale fully and expand laterally, try to use only your intercostal muscles. The hands should ever so slightly and slowly grow away from each other.

4. Exhale when inhalation is complete, relaxing the intercostals and letting the hands on your ribs come back towards the midline.

5. The emphasis is to try **not** to use the diaphragm or muscles of the upper chest, but to concentrate solely on the lower rib cage area.

6. If you find yourself having trouble with this isolation, try this alternative:

   a. Sit comfortably as you did in the preparatory exercise, and this time lean the torso slightly forward.

   b. Place the hands on the lower ribs as we did above, and draw the chin comfortably into the chest.

   c. In this shape, the bent torso restricts the diaphragm while the chin-to-chest helps hold back the upper chest.

7. As you build awareness and are comfortable, start with a three-second count in and out, maintaining an equal breathing rhythm, and gradually increase to five to ten seconds.

8. Ten rounds (one round is one inhale and exhale cycle) is recommended.

EXERCISE 4: CLAVICAL BREATHING (PART 3 OF 3)

Most people these days are quite capable of breathing into the upper chest—in fact for many it is the only area of the lungs they use. As you perform this exercise of isolating the upper chest region, note that this is still in fact one aspect of a deep breath. However, this region can have a far greater level of control when used slowly and deliberately as opposed to the automatic, rapid, and shallow breath most of us experience throughout the day. This exercise aims to isolates the set of muscles that controls the upper lungs for practice purposes only, and **not** to further the habit of only breathing in the upper chest.

1. Place one hand on your upper chest between your collar bones. Inhale by moving only the clavicle muscles of this region, and keeping the intercostals and diaphragm still as best you can.

2. Concentrate on the area below the armpits while keeping an equal count of breaths in and out.

3. To deepen the magnitude of this breath, inhale slowly and when you feel full continue for two more seconds, giving the alveoli of the lungs time to expand. You should be able to feel the tops of the lungs (near the base of the throat and neck) completely fill.

4. Release the breath and exhale, breathing out a few seconds longer than you think you possibly could so that the clavicle area is concave and emptied. It may help to cough gently to expel the air.

5. As you mature in the practice, there should be no pauses between inhale and exhale, even with these deeper breaths.

6. Use a count of two seconds in and out at first, and gradually increase the count to five to ten seconds over time.

7. Do ten rounds, again maintaining an equal count for inhalation and exhalation.

EXERCISE 5: THREE-PART BREATHING

For this exercise we simply use each of the three parts of the breathing process described above in a coordinated, fluid manner using all the muscles of the lungs for a deep, rhythmic breath. Inhale first into the base of the lungs (diaphragm) and then fill the intercostals area to the sides, finishing with the upper clavicle area. Without pausing, exhale from the clavicle area first, then draw the intercostals in second and finish by pulling the navel to the spine as the diaphragm expels the entirety of the breath.

Once the rhythmic breath is achieved, begin to concentrate on a smooth transition from inhalation to exhalation and vice-versa. Starting out, though it may be somewhat frightening at times, avoid the tendency to start each exchange quickly. Usually, a person breathes in too quickly for the first few seconds as there is a desire to get the air in; likewise, when beginning to exhale there is a tendency to expel the air forcefully at the beginning. Attempt to breathe to the best of your capability in a smooth, even fashion. In time and with practice, you may work up a count to help equalize the length of the inhalation and exhalation. This even, balanced breath is geared toward being the breathing pattern for meditation. A slow, steady breath keeps the thoughts slow and steady as well.

Exercise 6: Equal Breathing

Once established in three-part yogic breathing, the next step is to work on lengthening the breath and controlling the smooth transition when the breath changes from inhalation to exhalation and vice-versa. A helpful tool to facilitate this is counting the breath length.

1. Periodically, time your breathing rhythm as you breathe in and out of the nose. Fill each of the three areas of the lungs for an equal number of seconds, keeping it the same for inhalation and exhalation.

   a. For example: Someone might start working at a count of two; two seconds into the diaphragm, two seconds in the intercostals, and two seconds into the clavicle. The exhale would have the same pattern.

2. Over time, you may begin to work towards breathing in five seconds per each area of the lungs. This gives a fifteen-second inhalation and a fifteen-second exhalation. After six-months of practice, this is the level recommended for each person.

a. Please note, those with athletic or musical backgrounds may notice breathing patterns reaching thirty seconds in and out. This is a natural side effect of these other talents, but the key is to eventually reach fifteen seconds.

While there are numerous health benefits to a slow, steady breath, there are also mind-quieting effects of slow breathing. This exercise may be practiced for the duration of your life. To make things even better, larger quantities of carbon dioxide waste is eliminated from the lungs. This improves diaphragmatic functioning and ventilation effectiveness, allowing for a deeper, more nourishing in-breath.

Remember, smooth breathing is graceful. The lungs move in a fluid fashion while they slowly open. As the lungs expand the atmosphere encourages air to enter the lungs. If the lungs move in a jerky or tense fashion, the air enters abruptly and not to the fullest capacity. Pay attention to the flow of air into the lungs as a first step. Then, notice the transition of air after the inhalation and exhalation. Some may hold the breath after inhaling, while others may drop the chest and suddenly force the air out of the lungs. After exhaling, the abrupt tendencies are sudden inhalation and a pause followed by a gulping breath—both of which greatly decrease the efficiency of respiration.

BREATHING IN DAILY LIFE (BONUS EXERCISE!)

Once you learn deep breathing via meditation, it is a helpful tool to use whenever you feel stressed. Simply pause to center, and then begin expanding all of the areas of your lungs as you enjoy a deep breath. Simultaneously, consider a new perspective in the time that you are breathing, and discover a healthy way of dealing with the stressful situation.

You can even practice breathing while moving. As an exercise, practice walking very slowly while you concentrate on your breathing rhythm. Many meditation traditions perform meditative walking in between longer meditation sittings. Simply take very slow steps with keen awareness of your breath and of each micromovement you make on your walk. Remain very aware of your actions and breath, as well as the thoughts that arise. As you might imagine, you may apply this conscious approach to living to any activity in your daily life: cooking, walking, exercise, repetitive tasks … the list is really endless. Your breath is with you always from the moment you exist until you take your last—this very simple exercise allows you to use that to your advantage and growth.

Summary
(and Meditative Humor)

Please continue to breathe!

Seven

....

Relaxation

Sitting on a porch swing in the sunshine with a glass of lemonade evokes relaxation. Smelling the flowers in the garden or naming the puffy clouds passing by on a Sunday afternoon offers the simplicity of relaxation. The still waters of a pond invite quietude, and the rise and set of the sun inspire people from all cultures. In their natural state, everyday moments can be relaxing. Though pleasant to consider, sadly with the current state of the stressful world, the idea of simply relaxing brings along a myriad of complexities.

As you may expect from this program by now, actually achieving the goal is not as simple as just doing that activity. You are now on a journey to understand your stress, how and why you think, rediscover how you breathe, and now, learn to relax.

I have a few steps for you before outlining a host of relaxation exercises. Beyond giving you techniques, you must first find the time to actually relax. If you do not have any free time in your schedule, it will surely be hard to sit on the porch and contemplate your navel. Carving out a routine time for relaxation eventually dovetails with your chosen meditation time. Choosing a place to relax, simple as that seems, is an important aspect of psychological commitment. Next, there is checking your physical body for any areas of tension by stretching your spine in each of its five directions. Finally, the concept of "letting go" and forgiveness completes the relaxation prerequisites. After you have mastered these steps, you will be prepared to experiment with a host of relaxation exercises to settle on what ultimately resonates with and works for you.

Scheduling Time to Do Nothing

The Dalai Lama once said that "our [Tibetan Buddhism's] nothingness is something." Achieving a state of tranquility—your birthright—is some feat in the busy modern world. No amount of tips will help you out on this issue. I cannot tell you inspirational stories of how to make time for nothing. Our lives are a quest for achievement and success, are they not? Doing nothing sounds uninviting, boring, and even apathetic. However bliss, joy, and happiness resides in moments where you are completely content with where you are—there is nothing else that you would rather be doing. Imagine a time and space where just being aware of being alive was the goal of life.

You must make the choice right here and right now to turn off all the reasons of why you need to be here or there, to do this or that, to read this or that, or help Mr. and Mrs. So-and-So. **Decide on twenty minutes for your solitude and take back your life right now.**

This taking time back may challenge everything that you have been taught. You are a productive person, a kind person, a hard-working person—but what many of you have not been taught is that you need a period of solitude each day to remain sane, stay relaxed, facilitate meditation, and simply recharge. Turn off the TV, turn off the computer, do one less activity this week, whatever you have to do. Take some downtime.

Yes, we all have to do our jobs and care for our loved ones. However, we also need to make time for the maintenance of our mind. Science is continuing to support the power of quieting the mind for human sanity as well as for creativity and productivity. Make this downtime an appointment as necessary as if it were with the most important person you know or even with your higher power. Make this appointment unbreakable. If you miss your quiet time one day, no worries, just make it the next day or catch up before sleeping.

EXERCISE 1: TAKING BACK TIME!
This taking back your time exercise is the shortest exercise in this program and the single most important:

Please write in the time here: _____ am or _____ pm

Place for Your Meditation

My first meditation class occurred at a Zen Buddhist Temple in Kyoto, Japan. As an overseas student in college, my professor and fellow classmate neglected to inform me that meditation evening included a short lecture in the Japanese language followed by two forty-five minute sitting sessions. I began learning to meditate like a novice swimmer thrown into deep water with the instructor saying, "Now swim!" In this case, the Zen master said, "Now meditate!"

The Bhagavad Gita's sixth chapter, titled "The Path of Meditation," is one of the first descriptions of meditation practice written nearly two thousand years ago. In other words, meditation was practiced for thousands of years and certainly prior to the written word; prior to scientific study on brain chemistry. Meditation is included in every world religion.

> *Those who eat too much or eat too little, who sleep too much or sleep too little, will not succeed in meditation. But those who are temperate in eating and sleeping, work and recreation, will come to the end of sorrow through meditation. Through constant effort they learn to withdraw the mind from selfish cravings and absorb it in the Self. Thus they attain the state of union.*
> —*Bhagavad Gita,* Easwaran, chapter 6, verses 16–18

This quote for the modern person could be rewritten: "Those who rely on their computer, phone, or TV too much or those who neglect their responsibilities will not succeed in meditation. However, those who are balanced in their use of technology, those who get their sleep and have time for practice will find inner peace."

The place for practice may be any quiet place in your home. Make this place special during your meditation time by leaving a prop in that area to transform a normal living space into your personal retreat center. The bedroom or living room may transform in your mind by a prop like a candle, meditation cushion, or inspirational book placed in a strategic position.

Ideally, a consistent time for meditation creates a momentum as the body and mind habitually move into a quiet space over time. The most common times are early in the morning, before sleeping, or before dinner. Naturally, each person's life varies, but the key is to be as consistent as possible.

Length of practice depends on the person and what works best. Normally, twenty minutes is considered the minimum time for meditation that allows the mind to reach a level of quiet. However, five minutes each day is more valuable than sixty minutes one day a week.

Exercise 2: Setting the Stage

To continue in the theme of committing to a set routine of practice, make your choices of meditation props, timing, and place, and write them in the space provided below.

1. Choose your meditation place and prop.

2. Pick your time: ___ am/pm

3. Decide on the length of the practice: ___ minutes

Preparing the Body for Relaxation: Loosen the Spine; Stretch in Five Directions

In a technical definition, meditation concerns the quieting of the mind. The West defines the mind as the intellect relating to the brain. However, yoga defines the concept of mind by the term *citta*, which is often translated as mind-body complex. The holistic approach to viewing a human being means that the body is a part of the mind, just as the nervous system reaches from the brain to every muscle, organ, and gland in the body. By noticing the state of the physical body, you may simplify the process of meditation. When there is tension in the body, the mind will be disturbed slightly. By gentle stretching in the five directions that the spine may move, the body will begin the process of relaxation.

EXERCISE 3: STRETCHING THE SPINE IN FIVE DIRECTIONS (IN LESS THAN FIVE MINUTES)

While sitting in a chair, move the body in these directions. With each movement observe how your body feels. Stop if you feel any discomfort.

1. Upward

   Reach your arms above your head and stretch upward. Hold for ten seconds before lowering the arms, then repeat three times.

2. Sideward

   Place the right hand on the chair next to your thigh. Lean to the right and hold for ten seconds as comfortable. Return to center slowly, and then repeat three times on the right and left sides.

3. Forward

   First roll the head forward and relax the neck and shoulders. Then, lean forward to allow the spine to be exercised in a forward bend. Remain here for three to five breaths before slowly rolling back up.

4. Backward

Place both hands on the base of the chair while gently arching back. Be careful not to lean back on the chair but simply arch your back by leaning forward slightly before leaning backwards. Hold for five to ten seconds and slowly return the spine to neutrality.

5. Twisting

Reach the right hand to the left thigh and perform a gentle twist. Hold for ten seconds and then gently unwind, repeating three times on both sides.

The Mind of Relaxation: "Letting Go" and Forgiveness

Teaching my first class, I explained every detail about relaxation. By the end of the class I was exhausted. The teacher cannot do the relaxation for the student: only the person relaxing can master the relaxation. This, like all the steps in this book, represents a set of "how-to" instructions you have to discover. Discovery is an important aspect of being a student. As you make small strides in understanding, you feel excited because the discovery is your own and you earned it. You experienced the task in a manner uniquely your own.

The concepts of "letting go" and "forgiveness" cannot be adequately described in language. You must reflect on this topic and realize that the process of truly learning how to relax is a lifelong pursuit. Ironically, from wherever you begin your journey into relaxation, the slightest improvement feels like witnessing a new vista for the first time. In other words, the journey is truly remarkable as you discover, uncover, and peel away layers of stress to find internal harmony.

The term "letting go" relates to the small stuff in this context. "Let go" or release your daily burdens and for the moment, take a mental break. Stop fretting over small problems, step outside of your life, and feel the bigger picture. This differs from denial of problems; it is an exercise in shifting perspective on your life as a means of coping.

For example, take a fictional character, John, who today sat in thirty minutes of traffic because a tree fell onto the highway. His boss gave him a dirty look when he walked into the meeting late at which time he realized that his lunch was on the kitchen table at home. By the end of this particular day, a host of little things had gone wrong, but John had the presence of mind to pause and take some time to relax. In this process, he remembered all the events of this disorganized day. Each time, he creatively let them go. With each exhalation he let go of one of the daily difficulties. Within a few minutes there was nothing on his mind so he just fell into a quiet state for five minutes. Physically, he felt refreshed from the exercise, and mentally he was clear.

As you experiment with the exercises below, allow yourself the flexibility to devise your own method of letting go. One person who was part of my meditation classes years ago had a way of visualizing a bubble with its rainbowlike color surrounding all the things that she needed to release—and in good bubbly fashion, the problems just floated away. Another man had a method of repeating to himself a short mantra, "Thank you for this life," each time he thought of a stressful element of the day; it worked for him. Devise any strategy that works for **you**—let it be your personal style so long as you can "let go" of tension.

Forgiveness relates to much larger issues. If "letting go" is something the instructor can't do for the student, figure that teaching another how to forgive is by far a larger topic. Forgiveness can relate to one's self as well as to others. No matter how long your forgiveness list may be, it is a long-term process. Therefore it is common that while relaxing, the mind will dwell on anything that has yet to be truly forgiven. Since forgiveness is a very complicated and tender subject that cannot be taken lightly nor wished away by a creative relaxation exercise, please see if you can for the time being accept the fact that you, like most other human beings, have areas of life in need of forgiveness. This is not a denial, but rather permission to allow you to relax in the midst of an imperfect life. I have yet to meet someone who had an absolutely perfect life. The only individuals who seem to have perfect lives are those who have accepted life the way it is. They accept the shape of their nose, the proportions of their body, and realize it may take time to completely forgive hurtful moments.

The point herein is that it is possible for you to be simultaneously aware of difficulties in life *and* choose to accept those difficult areas of life. From this perspective you may relax even while in the traffic jam or while living in a world that has war, hunger, and prejudice. Begin by accepting yourself where you are right now—it is a big step of forgiveness of yourself and a huge key for relaxation and later meditation.

Simple Relaxation Exercises

There are hundreds of relaxation exercises that you may find via teachers, books, and the Internet. The exercises for relaxation are all effective for the type of person suited for that type of relaxation. The subtext for this book that recommends finding the meditation that works for you also applies to finding the type of relaxation that suits your needs. Below are several of exercises, all which are good, but they are in no way better than nor replacing any other practice you may have tried in your life. Please pick one or two exercises below that suit you and certainly do not expect to practice all of them. Relaxation is the goal, not trying every exercise that exists—worrying about how you decide to relax is counterproductive! And unlike the previous chapter on breathing exercises, there is no logical or implied progression of relaxation efforts. I cannot stress enough that it is more important to find your relaxation preference than trying everything others recommend.

Exercise 4: Relaxation Body Scan

You can use this as a baseline experience to see how the body feels and what level of relaxation is present.

1. To begin, find a comfortable position for you: sitting with the head supported, reclined slightly, or completely lying down.

2. Remain in this position practicing for up to ten minutes, any longer will often result in sleep. Note that if you do doze off, this is a natural cue that your body needs more sleep and that you might want to consider increasing your sleep time!

3. Start to slowly "scan" your body from the crown of your head to the soles of your feet, all the while observing a slow breath. This scanning can best be described as full awareness at whatever part of the body you have reached. In so doing, the feeling and sensations in those areas increase. Depending on the level of ease in each part of your body, this scan will clue you in to which muscles or joints are at ease and where tension may be hiding.

4. Continue to be a witness to your body and name "your body" instead "the body." For example, instead of saying "my shoulders are tense," say "the shoulders are tense." As the lungs exhale and release air, the neck releases; then the back releases and so forth. This language creates a more detached perspective that greatly assists in relaxation.

5. After you reach the soles of your feet, pause for a moment or two to integrate. If you are not feeling drowsy, you may repeat the scan up to two more times. See if you can allow the tense parts to relax a bit more on each subsequent scan.

Exercise 5: Relaxation on Intention

Connect a personal intention to your mind's responses to the body. You can use this as a powerful tool to release any tensions in the body. Please note that this differs from formal meditation because the mind is actively replaying the intention while you focus it through the body.

1. Simply lie in any comfortable position and begin repeating your personal life intention.

2. Allow all thoughts that may emerge in your mind to flow into your intention and be accepted by that spiritual intention. Allow any and all feelings that come up to be accepted and nurtured by the intention. Allow all tension to be healed by the intention. You can even use these instructions as a silent, mental mantra to help facilitate the process.

3. Start to feel a balance in yourself on all levels. Allow your senses to visualize, your emotions to feel, or your mind to think about the intention in a passive manner. This exercise is a perfect opportunity to understand your basic nature.

4. If you are having trouble with an intention that resonates with you, affirmations can be a temporary substitute. Some acceptable affirmations include, but are not limited to thefollowing as focal points for relaxation: compassion, peace, joy, thanksgiving, stillness, faith, confidence, courage, forgiveness ...

EXERCISE 6: SIMPLE SEATED RELAXATION

Traditional relaxation poses are in a supine position similar to that used for sleep. Most people associate lying down with relaxation, rest, or sleep. Likewise, there is an unspoken belief that sitting or standing upright equates to action as we tend to work either in a seated or standing position; the mind typically activates when upright.

Due to the association of action and upright posture, some people think that meditation is easier while lying. However, after eight to twelve minutes, most people fall asleep or lose their alertness—if you experimented with the above exercises, you may have noticed this for yourself! In order to associate alertness with passive consciousness, try to sit upright while doing a simple relaxation exercise.

1. Recline against a wall so your head is supported by the wall.

2. Begin to form a smile on your face, and then start to grin from ear to ear. Feel the smile travel throughout the body.

3. Gradually allow the smile to melt into the face leaving a peaceful grin. Then, mentally move the smile feeling to the forehead and release any lingering thoughts.

4. Allow the smile to penetrate the skull, and then begin to drop the smile down into the neck and shoulders.

5. Move the smile into the heart, and create a peaceful acceptance of emotions—do not be tempted to disguise emotions, simply feel the emotions with a peaceful awareness.

6. Feel the smile in the stomach region of the body, relaxing the diaphragm. Complete the exercise by letting the smile drift down the legs as you allow the feeling to continue. It is best to complete the exercise in eight to ten minutes.

Exercise 7: Relaxation on a Passage

Recite this passage (or use another such passage): "all things are changing" *(Anitya Bhavana)*. You may repeat the passage more than one time and read it slowly with pauses. Reflect on the meaning of the thoughts as a means of relaxation. The full text of the Anitya Bhavana is below. As you mature in the reflection on short passages, feel free to "test" yourself with longer passages. The complexity of the passage is not the emphasis—that your mind has a deep, spiritual meaning to reflect upon is.

> *What was in the morning is not at mid-day; what was at mid-day is not at night, for all things are transitory (anitya). Our body which is the cause of all kinds of human effort is as transitory as the scattering clouds. All our objects of pleasure are changing. Wealth is as transitory as a wave, youth like a cotton particle blown off in a whirlwind, and opportunities like fleeting dreams. Why should I be attached to anything when nothing is permanent and everything is changing?*

Exercise 8: Sixteen-Point Body *Marmasthanani*

This exercise is an ancient yogic practice that is just as effective in the modern world. *Marman* refers to "joint," or any of the several particularly vital spots in the body, particularly points centered around clusters of nerve endings where sensitivity is acute. Below you will find the full sixteen-point exercise, but you may also follow an abbreviated list at first if you have a hard time recalling the entire list.

This practice is best performed lying down and focusing on each area for about thirty seconds, resulting in a practice that takes eight to twelve minutes. Remember not to go over twelve minutes or it is likely that you will fall asleep. As many of us are mildly sleep deprived (if not outright having insomnia), often you will doze off because your body needs the rest. Always remember, that is perfectly acceptable! Get the rest and consider it a sign that you might need to get to bed earlier or reduce the number of activities in your schedule. Below are the points with some simple instructions to further guide the exercise:

1. Tips of the toes, for the feet and legs to be grounded.

2. Ankles, for freedom to spring forward.

3. Knees, for the pressure from holding the body in place.

4. Fingertips, for the arms and wrists.

5. Tailbone, for the anus area and lower back.

6. Lower belly, for deep breathing.

7. Navel, for the reproductive area.

8. Stomach, for peaceful digestion and the internal visceral organs.

9. Heart, to soften the chest muscles.

10. Throat, to target the neck and shoulders with the throat's softness.

11. Lips, to release jaw tension.

12. Tip of the nose, to open the sinus area and release irritation.

13. Eyes, to move inward and relax the temples.

14. Third eye, to value being passive and being receptive.

15. Forehead, to let worry pass and release excessive thinking.

16. Top of the head, to connect the entire body.

EXERCISE 9: RELAXATION TO MUSIC

This exercise is relatively simple: from a comfortable position, simply listen to a soothing piece of music and allow relaxation to occur naturally. Generally instrumental music without vocals is recommended as recognition of vocal sounds triggers the mind. For some individuals, chanting or vocalization of a foreign tongue can have the same effect. The music you choose is largely a matter of preference, so listen to your own responses to a particular musical choice to see if it really is a good facilitator of relaxation. Please note that if you are musically inclined, this may be a difficult exercise as the mind may naturally wish to analyze the music. If it does, do not be alarmed; simply cultivate awareness and see if the mind slows on its own.

1. As you sit with the music, allow all thoughts to pass without judgment.

2. Allow and observe the mind as it becomes still—it will take some time.

3. Allow yourself to just be in the moment with the music.

4. Unlike some of the other exercises, do not even put emphasis on your breath.

5. Allow yourself to release the dependence you have on your senses for a few moments, even your hearing, and let yourself sink deeply into the enveloping music.

6. As the music continues, withdraw inward away from your senses that direct you outward.

7. When the music ends, pause for a moment in silence. The silence after a sound is just as important—if not more so—than the sound that precluded it. Enjoy those moments.

Exercise 10: Guided Relaxation Focusing on the Exhalation

Unlike the lying or seated relaxations above, this exercise has you instead lie on your stomach in Crocodile Pose (instructions on how to get into the pose will follow). In this position, the belly is completely supported and sinking into the earth. This "pressure" allows for a slight resistance to inhalation, bringing with it greater awareness to the process. Perhaps more importantly, it facilitates a much deeper exhalation.

Come to the floor on your belly with the tops of your feet on the earth and bring your big toes together, ankles moving apart. For some this may be uncomfortable so feel free to experiment with bringing the heels together instead and letting the toes turn out. Bring your arms forward and form a little pillow to support your head in any comfortable fashion: forehead on the hands, chin on the hands, or cheek on the hands—though be sure to alternate the cheek so as not to cramp one side of the neck over the other. If you feel at all uncomfortable on your stomach, the next best suggestion is to lie on your side (for example, some very thin people may experience discomfort as their hip points could dig into the earth, while others may feel excessive tenderness in either the chest, lower back, or both).

1. From this position, focus on a slow, deliberate exhalation.

2. Allow the layers of tension in your body to release with each full exhalation. The emphasis here is of course on the "full," such that subsequent inhalations are even more deep and revitalizing.

3. Notice how the weight of the body promotes the feeling of a sigh as you exhale. Use that sighing effect to let go of any held tension or resistance.

4. Continue to breathe into the belly as well as the intercostals of the chest.

5. Envision and then begin to feel a wave of energy emanating from your core as your breath travels throughout the body.

EXERCISE 11: RELAXATION ON COLOR

For those with a very visual disposition or with a vivid imagination, the use of color can be a powerful tool for relaxation.

1. Begin in any comfortable relaxation pose that you have experimented with.

2. Visualize a color that soothes you. Begin to relate the chosen color to a particular aspect of nature that resonates with you.

3. Be creative with the color and what it is doing. Let it fill you, surround you or penetrate deep into your heart...

4. Sit with the color and the energy the color provides for up to ten minutes.

EXERCISE 12: RELAXATION OF LETTING GO!

Sometimes when we sit down to relax, no matter how hard we try and how much we have been meditating, the thoughts of our minds just keep jumping up and preventing us. The act of surrendering to a higher power can help encourage the mind to relinquish its fickle thoughts. A favorite means of mine is to imagine that you are floating on a river. You float very safely and can feel the gentle current of the water in the slow drifting and meandering. As you drift on, a basket slowly floats up beside you and allows you to place any worries, concerns, or issues that weigh on your mind. Notice that you will take a break from these issues as you mentally place them in the basket.

Continue breathing and floating as you feel thoughts and tensions release with each exhalation. When new issues arise, continue to place those in this basket, for no matter how many thoughts come up, the basket is never more than half full. Allow yourself to temporarily let go of past hurts, regrets, and resentments. As you place these issues in the basket one by one, notice how you feel while remaining passively aware.

Continue breathing and floating as you steadily feel a deeper state of relaxation. At the end of the relaxation, your perception will alter slightly, helping you understand the issues in the basket from a new perspective. You neither denied these issues nor dwelled on them; you allowed a sense of acceptance of life to soothe the body with relaxation.

Exercise 13: Relaxation with an Open Mind

This traditional relaxation exercise is simply lying still until the body and mind quiet. There are no instructions or techniques beyond self-observation and questioning. We tend to practice this relaxation in the Corpse Pose lying down on your back (supine) as we symbolically practice surrendering the entire body and mind to the nothingness of complete relaxation.

1. Contemplate who you *really* are beyond your body and mind.

2. Examine who is *really* doing the relaxation:

   - Is it the ego?

   - Is it me, the author?

   - Is it the meditation tradition's wisdom?

   - Is it any ambient sounds in the environment around you?

   - Is it the breath?

   - Is the mystery of it all the key?

3. Continue to surrender yourself as thoughts reappear.

Eight

....

Nutrition

The Buddha preached the middle path, meaning living a balanced life devoid of extremes. Likewise, "neither eat too much nor eat too little" is a quote found from the Meditation section in the Bhagavad Gita. Common sense prevails that eating too much beyond the weight gain potential brings on a sleepy person because the body has to process a large amount of food, and as you can imagine, a sleepy person has trouble meditating! Likewise, a person who does not eat enough food may be very trim and even have a clear mind, however eventually weakness will cause the mind to be incapable of maintaining concentration. Finding balance with nutrition is an important step for not only overall wellness but meditation as well.

Balanced Body, Balanced Mind

Continuing with this book's theme of discovering your type of meditation and understanding how to adapt a personal practice to your lifestyle, the goal in this chapter is to gain awareness of how your nutrition choices affect your mind. Notice that the intention is NOT to specify a dietary prescription on what to eat. The goal herein is to offer guidelines for you to examine how different kinds of food affect your mind. Each person's body reacts differently to foods. Depending on your daily activity and current stage of life, your nutritional needs will vary.

To establish a baseline for this chapter, please fill out a dietary journal to see how your diet affects your mind. In the chart below, notice how a meal's effect on the mind is questioned. This type of awareness expands beyond the normal caloric approach to nutrition.

Exercise 1: Food Journal

Keep a journal of your diet for three days. Throughout the day, record all the foods and beverages you eat and drink, the time of day you ate, the associated emotions during eating, and if possible, the feeling after eating. Use the model as demonstrated in the chart below to begin to understand your relationship with food in a deeper fashion. The goal of this part of the journal is to reveal unconscious patterns. By remaining conscious of your eating choices, you may bring more balance into your mind. Try to stay focused on increased awareness versus judging yourself as a "good" or "bad" eater. Simply learn from the experience of how foods affect your mind and body. Eating habits take time and persistence to change.

Often times when students fill out the food diary, the diary itself becomes the teacher. By moving to a "witness" perspective regarding your food choices, you may see objectively what the good beliefs about food are and which beliefs you hold that are more detrimental to you personally. Please note that if you have a serious health condition, you should always consult with a medical professional before making any changes to diet, just like you would any other lifestyle change. This book does not advocate anything beyond common sense to increase the quality of one's diet. There is no prescription for one diet formula or type of food.

EXAMPLE FOOD JOURNAL:

Time	Food	Energy	Emotions	Intellect	Spiritual
7 am	Lemon water	Slow to awaken	Tenuous, big day ahead	Foggy	Apprehensive
8 am	Toast	Brighter	Ready to meet the day	Clearer after meditation	Accepting
etc...					

Feeding the Whole Person

A second perspective that relates to viewing meditation as a complete lifestyle applies this philosophy to your nutrition. In other words, nutrition may be considered more than just proteins, carbohydrates, minerals, vitamins, and water.

In Western culture, an entire industry revolves around dieting or weight loss. People wish to be slim for a variety of reasons, such as personal image, better energy, or longevity. Each of these goals may or may not lead to spiritual fulfillment depending on how a person makes use of improved health. Understanding nutrition as feeding the entire human being is found in the *Taittiriya Upanishad*; in fact, this is one of the first places in recorded history (dated around 500 BCE) that talks about food and well-being in a cosmic fashion:

> *Whatsoever beings live on this earth, truly they are born from food, also they remain alive on food alone and in the same way they return to it at the end. Food is, verily, the first among all that is created, therefore it is said to be the medicine for all. One who meditates on food as Brahman, surely obtains all food.*
>
> —*Taittiriya Upanishad,* 2:1

In this text, verses two to six outline the essence of good health in terms of five sheaths (*koshas*) that surround pure consciousness. This paradigm moves from the gross physical body to subtle concepts of energy and bliss in telescopic fashion. Through this progression you are led from the external physical reality into the pure spiritual experience of divine consciousness. In other words, you eat to nourish your spirit. The five sheaths demonstrate that a subtler counterpart guides each level of consciousness. In this conceptual framework, each element is related to the other and we are guided to reach the highest aspirations of the divine reality via nutrition of the total human being. By relating nutrition to all areas of your life, anything you consume—from apples to emotions—counts as whole-person food.

Body: Take notice of the effects that various foods have on the mind. Certain foods that are easy to digest and provide bountiful nutrition affect the mind in positive ways. Foods that are relatively toxic to the body are to be avoided as much as possible with regard to quieting the mind. Decrease processed foods including trans fats, refined sugars, caffeine, soda, and alcohol. Increase whole foods that agree with your constitution.

Energy: Actively improving your energy feeds the body by aiding in digestion, assimilation, and excretion of food. Breathing exercises are very helpful, as are forms of exercise. Aerobic exercise and outdoor living are very good for overall health of the body and mind. Notice if you feel more vitality and alert with energy for meditation.

Mind/Emotion: Notice your emotional intake. First, notice how you are reacting to situations based on your lack of understanding. Remember, you have control of your emotional reactions to situations and your emotional food may be regulated by your reactions, be they pure or disturbed. Try to minimize repeatedly charged situations that cause a disturbed mind. Be sure to take time to enjoy positive emotions with laughter, fun, and free time. Performing a relaxation exercise each day may help rebalance emotions and provide healthy emotional food. A good lesson for emotions is that everything has its own nature. For example, the nature of a car is for the tires to wear out every few years, so why should we get emotional when we get a flat tire? In the case of persistent emotional upsetting over a serious interpersonal situation, it is generally good practice to consult with a counselor or other type of support.

Intellect: The intellect finds new ideas stimulating. Human beings who are in a state of constant learning remain youthful, sharp, and open-minded. However, the intellect does not need overstimulation via information. The intellect runs on clarity and simplicity. Be careful to monitor your electronic stimulation via telephones, cell phones, computers, Internet use, television, and other media. Overstimulation of the intellect clogs meditative clarity.

Spirit: Spiritual foods vary drastically, so please take the time to honor and discover how you feel fed spiritually. Common venues for spiritual food are in spiritual company, such as where a group of people intentionally join together to discuss spiritually related topics. Time spent in nature as well as time at organized religious activities may offer spiritual food. Personal prayer can sometimes feed the spirit as well as chanting, spiritual reading, and reflection. Simple living has an inherent spiritual quality whereas overscheduling tends to sacrifice time for spirituality.

EXERCISE 2: FEEDING THE WHOLE PERSON

Below are listed the five categories of the entire person. Notice your intake on those areas as well as any steps that you would like to increase.

1. **Food:** As in exercise 1, notice how foods affect your energy level, mood, intellect, and spirit. By learning from your experiences, you may determine ways to improve your diet.

2. **Energy:** Typically, physical exercise (when not overexerting) boosts energy levels. Try to do outdoor activities when possible. Deep breathing exercises and yoga postures are especially helpful for energy. Make a choice to exercise on a daily basis.

3. **Emotion:** This includes the intake of positive feelings as well as your reactions to situations. First, consider whether mundane activities are building up a positive reservoir of energy. List the types of activities that are uplifting to your emotions, like keeping in touch with friends, playing with kids, enjoying the sunrise and sunset, etc. If you have trouble with your list, start with simple things like a good meal or the kindness of your friends and family.

   Secondly, notice any situations where you overreact. Examine your reasons and see if you can balance your emotions by personal reflection. In the case of difficult or intensely stressful situations, it is usually best to attempt to find some helpful counsel from a professional trained in these matters. Finally, reduce any negative emotional input from sources like the media and negatively charged dynamics.

4. **Intellect:** Notice how new lessons or ideas permeate your intellect, reminding you to greet life with openness. With a clearer intellect, the mind's emotions are stabilized due to clear thinking. See how meditation or mind quieting exercises clear the intellect and give way to a clear mind.

5. **Spirit:** Notice if you already have a routine practice like walking in nature, attending religious services, prayer reading or a spiritual book that inspires you (among other examples). This type of inspiration empowers you to live with vitality in the midst of a chaotic world, distinguishing spiritual from intellectual.

Water, the Source of Life

Proper fluid intake is another basic aspect of nutrition that is still misunderstood by many people. Many health food regimens recommend six to eight glasses of water be consumed in a day. Noticing a light yellow color to the urine can be another indicator of neither drinking too little water (urine with dark yellow or orange tint) or over consuming water (clear urine). However, similar to the wisdom shared in this text in multiple places, the amount of water required per person to support healthy functioning depends upon a variety of factors. First is the geographic location in which you live, as well as the season. Second is the type of diet you eat. For example, the person who eats a diet high in vegetables and fruits needs less water due to the foods' water content. Third is the amount of activity you perform during your day.

Finally, there are drinks that have a paradoxical water-absorbing or dehydrating effect. Coffee, caffeinated teas, colas, sugary drinks, juices, and alcoholic drinks, although they contain water, have diuretic effects on the body. This means that the body secretes more water in the process of assimilating these types of beverages than received. Milk requires water for digestion and is considered more of a food than a beverage.

Drinks that are hydrating are plain water, herbal teas, mineral waters, or drinks mixing 1 ounce of fruit juice with 8 ounces of water. Herb teas are very diverse and offer hundreds of flavors (if you consider herbal combinations) that are all very good for your health.

Please note that an awareness of your fluid intake is very important. If you drink too much water, your body can wash out and ultimately dilute essential ions and minerals. If not enough water is consumed, your body will dry up, so to speak. As in all things, do your best to strike a balance and consult your nutritionist or doctor if you have any physical conditions.

The Mind-Body Digestion Link

Good digestion is a key to radiant health. The digestive system is a very sensitive mirror of the mind. Digestion is governed by the limbic area of the brain, largely under our subconscious control. Emotions and mental processes act directly on the limbic area of the brain, and via the nervous system, these processes affect the stomach and digestive organs. Thus, the digestive system is solely under the influence of the autonomic nervous system. The parasympathetic branch (the mode of the autonomic nervous system that is dominant in a relaxed state) turns on digestive juices, speeds up peristalsis (the rhythmic contractions of the lining of our digestive system) and opens the sphincters. Conversely, the sympathetic branch, or stress response, inhibits digestion.

> *The mind is like a sea, the body is the land and their sphere of interaction is the shore. When the mind is peaceful and relaxed, the sea is calm. When the mind is troubled the sea becomes turbulent and waves beat against the shore, tearing away large sections of the land. This is the psychosomatic process that results in indigestion, constipation, ulcers, diarrhea, and other major and minor diseases.*
>
> *—Unknown*

Before Eating:

· Come to the table relaxed and with awareness.

· Practice deep breathing to become more relaxed if necessary. Breath should be slow and rhythmical while eating.

· Take a moment of silence in gratitude for where the food came from, or say a few words of grace.

During a Meal:

· When commencing a meal, remain aware of your body, breath, and mind.

- Imagine that you are eating with your favorite deity, teacher, or simply your higher self.

- Try to sit cross-legged in Easy Pose or if you are in a chair, try not to cross your legs to let energy flow freely into the abdomen.

- Remain fully aware of the process of chewing and swallowing. Each taste, temperature, and texture should be fully experienced.

- Savor each bite slowly.

- Avoid watching TV or engaging in lengthy, high-energy conversations.

- Chew your food between ten and forty times before swallowing it, allowing digestive juices in the mouth to fully interact with each bite as you enjoy its flavor.

- Experience the meal with full awareness: the pleasure of eating, the comfort of having plenty (but not too much) and the energizing lightness that comes when the stomach is satisfied but not too full.

- Let go of fear (of weight gain or loss, eating too much, being perfect or imperfect).

After Eating:

- Remain aware that the food has passed down into your stomach and the digestive process is underway.

- Sense the effects the meal is having on your overall energy and perception of well-being.

With regard to diets and food choices, it is important to maintain a relaxed attitude and make changes slowly. Fast changes from a meat diet to vegetarianism may have worse results than a slow change to a natural diet that allows the body to adapt. Strict rigidity with diet may cause tension. Following the 90% rule can be very helpful: eat 90% pure and as long as one does not overeat, the other 10% can be what you like. The mind is not poisoned by an imperfect diet—it is poisoned by rigid beliefs.

The Relationship Between Food and the Mind

The discussion of pure thoughts in juxtaposition with positive and negative thoughts in chapter 5 used a paradigm that can be correlated to the effect of food on the mind. As you make different food choices, notice the effect those choices have on your energy levels as well as your mind. Whenever feeling particularly good or bad at any given time during the day, ask yourself, "What have I eaten?" and begin to find connections between your food choices with your state of mind. Notice how making pure choices begets balanced energy and more healthy choices. Likewise, notice how making poor choices begets poor energy and more unhealthy choices. Choices are self-perpetuating, like feedback loops in electrical and biological systems. Let your newfound awareness inform your dietary needs.

Again, I do not give you any absolute recommendations beyond the basic common sense strategy of self-awareness and whole-food nutrition. Foods considered empty of health benefits are not as recommended. Overly processed foods like refined sugar (including cane sugar, fructose, corn syrup, etc), white flour, soft drinks, excessive caffeine, alcohol, trans fats, and all junk foods are going to make the mind less alert over time. Our main common sense observance is to notice the mind especially after eating food that fits into the junk food category.

Nine

Sensory Mastery

One day while meditating on my breath I heard a seagull's squawk off in the distance. The squawk was an ordinary sound that reminded me of my grandparents' beach cottage. I could see the grey wall boards of the cottage behind the ocean mist. I remembered the family dinners on the glass table and the rickety wooden chairs. The salt of the ocean was refreshing on my skin as were spending precious moments with my grandfather as we would walk on the sandy beach. Literally, every year of my life, there are photos of me at this house, from a few months old to that one day...You may wonder why now in the middle of a meditation book am I going on and on about my grandparents' beach house?

I am trying to prove the point that, for an entire thirty-minute meditation session, I swam in the fond memories of that house. I even left out the trips to the boardwalk, the hurricane story, surfing, and staying with my cousins for weeks at a time. When I finally opened my eyes, I realized that there were noisy motorcycles everywhere and a few mango trees with one papaya tree mixed in between a series of buildings illustrated with yogic images. Yes, I was meditating in India, distracted by one seagull's squawk and completely forgetting the exercise of meditating on my breath!

Sensory Distraction While Meditating

In the example I just related, the daydream was triggered by one sound, but then all of my other senses participated. I smelled the air, visualized the grey wall boards, remembered the tasty meals, and felt the texture of the sand beneath my feet. All of that was a true story recounted from my memory.

Not all was lost during this distraction. Had I chastised my mind for being distracted and thought I had just wasted a precious meditation session in India, I would have made a strong negative imprint on my mind. However, the feeling of the daydream was very peaceful and full of appreciation. It signaled to me that I was feeling homesick: this was the first summer of my life where there would not be a visit to the beach with my grandparents and cousins. Even though I was twenty-five at the time, this was how my psyche expressed my feelings. I used this as a signal to attempt to write a few postcards to honor those homesick feelings.

This story has a few other silver linings. I have not yet told you the number of sounds I allowed to pass by my consciousness that day. For example, there were loud crows squawking incessantly during all my meditations in India along with rickshaws, noisy motorcycle-powered taxis; not to mention the occasional sounds of people talking or airplanes overhead. These sounds were practice for the exercise on understanding the sense of hearing discussed later.

Distractions occur for many reasons—far too many reasons to list here—so please make note of your own personal distractions as we move through the five senses. Discover how your mind works, how you relate to the senses, and which senses seem to trigger the most errant thoughts. Undoubtedly, one top distraction relates to pressing issues on your mind. The mind will use the senses as an excuse to daydream about your present concerns. A second major reason for sensory distractions is the opposite of the first, the mind will use sensory phenomenon as a reason to avoid meditating. This avoidance is a defense mechanism. While quieting your mind may sound and feel delightful, the journey to the quietude forces you to move through, understand, and release discomfort. And while on many days the mind may quiet quickly, there will be phases of your life where the quieting process is very difficult. I talk about how to cope with those more difficult moments because those times are when you need meditation the most.

The Benefits of Sensory Mastery

Think of an annoying sound and notice how your feel when that annoying sound attacks you. You would give in to the child's demand when she figured out how to work you over with that high pitched scream or her cutest-ever-sounding "pleeeeeeeease." Or think of how you cannot seem to resist eating all the cookies when you smell the bakery aroma, accompanied by regret afterwards. Whatever sense you think controls you really does not control you at all. In fact, your mind is just programmed in such a way that you think you must behave a certain way when that trigger activates.

Imagine understanding why you are programmed the way you are and then disengaging that program. Thus, the person who grunts at you at work would no longer bother you. The kids screaming would be kids screaming and not feeling as though you are going nuts (and then feeling guilty about going nuts and being in trouble with your spouse for promising treats again ...). Imagine that you could just eat one cookie and not beat yourself up afterwards. Imagine that you could meditate and remain undisturbed by each and every sound. Sound impossible? I assure you that it can be done. It requires some practice, but this little known set of teachings from the yogic path's preliminary teaching on meditation (*Pratyahara* is the official name of this set of practices) offers you a way to become free from sensory slavery.

The Nuance of Quieting the Senses

Exercises on the senses have both internal and external aspects. The actual exercises listed here relate to the physical working or external phase of the sense. The internal aspects of the senses are the mind's eye or the mind's interpretation of the sensory input. Directions for fully understanding and correcting the internal function of the mind are very difficult to explain in a book because your experience is unique. Similar to my story above on the beach house, my internal reason for being distracted by the seagull was homesickness. Unpacking the particular reasons for the homesickness is as complicated as my psyche. What led me to study overseas when yoga and meditation were considered an oddity by my family and peers? Why did I care so much about family that I was homesick? There is no one stock answer for these questions, and your journey will be just as unique. Stopping the exploration at the insight of feeling homesick would only stop the understanding at the top layer of the story to the loss of those layers beneath.

The only generalization I can make is not very general: your journey will be as unique as your DNA. What I can give you are a set of guidelines to help you understand yourself (these teachings are also found in *The Pure Heart of Yoga*, 155).

Steps to Minimize or Eliminate Sensory Distraction

1. Name the sensory disturbance.

2. Notice the details related to this input in terms of intensity, quality, and frequency.

3. Notice your feeling or emotional reaction to this disturbance.

4. Understand the roots of the feeling or emotion. Why do you react in a disturbed fashion to this stimulus?

5. Accept the possibility that the stimulus could be interpreted differently.

6. Create a positive or reality-based response to the stimulus.

7. Release the negative association, and reestablish a new relationship to this stimulus.

These steps foreshadow the process that will be applied to each of the five senses with exercises and examples. Notice that you will find that certain senses cause you more disruption than other senses. Typically, sounds are most disturbing for meditation, and sight is a close second. The three lesser sensory distractions are taste, touch, and smell; however exercises for each of these senses are included below.

Sound Perception

Begin by listing the sounds that typically bother you. Hold on to this list as you study your perception. The first step is to remove negative associations with the sound and recognize that it is just a sound, a neutral phenomenon. The same lawn mower that bothers one person may bring a smile to someone else's face. Sounds are just a part of nature; they are neither good nor bad. Some sounds are louder than others, and some sounds are persistent, but none give us an instruction to be annoyed. When we program our perception properly, the sound of a young child whining incessantly is no different than the sound of the wind whistling through the trees. Our value system determines the meaning of the sound. No one jumps when an airplane flies overhead but it can be just as noisy as the neighbor's loud lawn mower.

EXERCISE 1: FOCUS ON ONE SOUND
Find a consistent sound. In summertime, the chirp of one particular bird or the choir of crickets at night may suffice, depending on the time of day. Another common sound might be the hum of a machine or passing cars. Any sound will do, as long as it is consistent. If there is no continuously occurring sound, use an instrumental piece of music and isolate one instrument within the music. Focus your attention on the

sound and then notice how other sounds pull your attention from the mind and disturb your concentration. Once you have started to master this exercise, it can also be done during relaxation. Concentrate for five to ten minutes on this exercise.

Stage 1: The first stage of this exercise is to simply focus on the sound and maintain consistent concentration (no daydreaming). The second step is to recognize when and how the mind wanders to think about other errant sounds. If a truck drives by, how many thoughts did the mind make before returning to the original seed sound? Be patient and nonjudgmental with this second step, as it may require some time to master.

Stage 2: The next step to move further into understanding your responses to distraction would be to notice why certain sounds grip your mind's attention and others do not. Be an observer in this process. Pay attention to your feelings even if those feelings do not make sense at the moment. Why does one errant sound stir an emotional response and another one does not? Stay with that feeling and see what it means to you. Each time a new level of self-understanding burgeons, a new level of mastery of the senses occurs.

Stage 3: With practice, moments of unbroken concentration can happen for one to three or more minutes at a time. At this proficient stage, you can begin to work on the sounds that you find annoying in daily life. Apply this same process to the neighbor's dog yapping or the sounds of rush-hour traffic and discover that you can consciously ignore the sounds.

Stage 4: The fourth and final stage of the listening exercise occurs when you can listen to one sound and not react to other sounds that used to be disturbing. While listening to a sound and the telephone rings, the mind would simply notice the phone ringing and let the sound vibrate through the eardrum with no reaction. The sound is noticed but there are no thoughts attached to the sound. The attention remains fixed on the task at hand.

EXERCISE 2: RELAXATION TO MUSIC

Simply listen to a soothing piece of music and allow relaxation to occur naturally. While this exercise was highlighted during the relaxation chapter of the book (chapter 7), for some people this practice will also be very calming for the senses. Note that this is different from the above exercise as you will passively listen to the music and focus on the body. In the exercise above, the body is let go and only the mind is considered.

1. Allow all thoughts to pass without judgment.

2. Allow and observe the mind as it becomes still; it takes time.

3. Allow yourself to be.

4. Do not put emphasis on your breath.

5. Allow yourself to release the dependence you have on your senses for a few moments.

6. Let the thoughts pass without judgment, let the mind just "be," and avoid giving thought to the breath you take.

7. Just withdraw inward away from your senses that direct you outward.

Sight Perception

It is helpful to allow the eyes to perceive a situation based on the premise that there is always, yes always, more to a situation than the senses can perceive. When we understand that the senses are not foolproof, we react slowly to gather more information about a situation. Meditation helps one realize that even the mind does not comprehend reality fully.

The same type of distraction that occurs via sounds and hearing can happen through sight. While meditating, it is common for the eyes to continuing looking to and fro. Many of us think using imagery and therefore the eyes move rapidly even with the eyelids closed.

Perhaps a picture on the wall is crooked and it becomes bothersome to see it and not be able to correct it. A variety of thoughts and disturbances occur from ancillary visual input. The distracted mind moves from the discomfort of the crooked picture to memories, impulsive thoughts, and then other concerns or worries. See the exercises below to further the discussion with practice.

EXERCISE 3: SIGHT AND SPACE

The space exercise emphasizes a conscious gaze at nothing; yes, a looking at open space. When you can accomplish this exercise, you will learn how to physically step away from visual sensory input. Few of us have ever been taught that we do not have to think about everything our eyes see. Some artists have learned this skill but few laypeople have ever been instructed. This exercise gives some external control to the eyes and actually improves eyesight due to the relaxation effects.

Sit in a comfortable posture with your back erect and shoulders relaxed. The exercise symbol is made by joining the tip of the thumb and index finger to form two circular shapes in each hand. The other three fingers are kept straight. Bring the hands together so that the right and left fingertips touch. Turn the hands to be able to view the two circles created by the thumb and index finger unions. Like the name of this exercise suggests, the task is to look at space. The human eye perceives objects, so some directions are necessary to explain how to see space—to see nothing—and accomplish abstraction.

While in a comfortable seated pose with the hands joined, the first step is to see the center point of each of the circles simultaneously. Because the eyes cannot focus on two points at once, focus solely on the space between the fingers. At first, the eyes will dart from one hand to the other and not reach the type of seeing termed a gaze. Once that's accomplished, work with the awareness and divert the conscious attention from the outside object of space to an internal object of space.

1. While keeping the eyes on the hands, bring your conscious attention from the hands back to the eyes, the temples, and the area around your eyes. Notice how the physical eyes feel.

2. Relax the muscles around your eyes; this creates a more passive use. The eyes receive information so there is no need to strain or look actively. Practice looking passively.

3. Next, relax deeper by moving the awareness behind the eyes into your brain.

4. Find a quiet place within the heart area. Gradually drift from the head into the heart area, and perceive spaciousness there. The eyes remain fixed on the hands, but the awareness is inside.

5. Do not to strain the eyes in this exercise. Discontinue or practice a softer method of looking at the space so that the eyes are relaxed instead of active.

6. Once this is accomplished, imagine the space between all the things that are perceived normally.

7. After a few minutes close the eyes and continue to delve into your self by focusing on space. The result is to find the place behind the five senses, not only the eyesight.

8. To conclude, treat your eyesight gently. Gradually look around but consider this ending step as still a part of the exercise. Be careful not to startle yourself. In time, you will be able to turn your eyes on and off as you learn to gaze and recognize that you do not need to see nor know everything.

EXERCISE 4: CANDLE GAZING

Candle gazing is an ancient art that serves to quiet the mind. To start, sit about twenty inches from a lit candle with the flame placed at eye level. If for some reason candle gazing is prohibitive, you can substitute a landscape or the blue sky to gaze at. Be in a room free of strong air currents to ensure that the flame burns straight up. Avoid eye strain and consult with an optometrist if you have any preexisting eye conditions. Look at the flame and notice your first interpretation of it. Continue looking at the flame and examine it from the following perspectives:

- Note your first perception of the flame and name it.

- Relax the eyes and temples, and notice the flame.

- Observe deep breathing while viewing the flame.

- Feel your heart while looking at the flame.

- Ignore everything in your field of view except for the flame.

For most candle gazers, the flame is seen from a variety of angles. The flame will seem small at certain times and then larger at other times. The flame's essence is felt in other moments. Add your own observations to the variety of responses and notice that your eyes perceive a limited field of reality.

If the limited nature of the sense of sight can be internalized, then the seer ("see-er") never stops seeing. Flames, as well as other objects are seen as a complex aspect of nature. Often vast individual assumptions are made from eyesight alone. Imagine what life could be if you saw things as they connect to the greater whole. The gazing exercise could also be applied to the facial expressions of a human being in order to recognize the truth in not judging a book by its cover. If no human being truly understands him or herself, how can an observer expect to make broad insights from eyesight alone?

After working with this exercise over time, the gazer gains an understanding that a relaxed, soft gaze takes in more than a strained stare. Eyes that dart to and fro or that are squinty and tense constrict the nervous system. A soft gaze greatly reduces nervous strain and enhances concentration. In a yoga pose practice, maintaining a soft gaze with the eyes open or closed is always recommended. When sensory distractions are removed, thought distractions are also minimized.

During meditation, the ability of gazing may be applied to any visual stimulus that distracts the mind. If you are meditating and you start to see things or colors, you can simply allow an internal gaze to cease the looking. This brings the mind back to the meditation topic. Similar to the sense of hearing, there may be a deeper issue that causes the eyes to be distracted even while closed in meditation. Each person has to understand the roots of the thought patterns that drive the senses.

Taste, Touch, and Smell Perception

The senses of taste, touch, and smell are lesser distractions during seated meditation practice. While aromas associate the mind with strong memories, these situations are less frequent when meditating. Likewise, the hands and skin are typically passive during meditation practice. If you have any special reasons to explore these two senses, follow the same process of understanding the meaning of your responses to them and you will be able to find freedom from them.

Taste is largely abated by placing the tip of the tongue softly on the upper palate (clef) behind the front two upper teeth. The tongue placement (*mudra*) seals or closes the sense of taste while also symbolically sealing the action of speech. Taste plays a larger role in terms of diet during the observation of a healthy lifestyle.

Exercise 5: Cultivating Taste Awareness

1. Notice you attachment to the flavors of certain foods in the same manner discussed with sight and sound.

2. Examine how the mind interprets the taste of the food you are eating. Are you actually tasting or just gulping it down?

3. Are you merely savoring the flavor but tasting it only as a means of avoiding how you feel?

4. Are you misinterpreting the taste of a food that has no nutritional value as something that is healthy?

Mastering the Five Senses

Once you have begun to gain some sensory awareness, you can learn to drift to a place beyond the five senses. Meditation may be divided into levels. As the mind is an intangible thing it is very difficult, but mastering the level of sensory distraction is a level that few meditators are taught. The above exercises, while simple, straightforward, and relatively manageable are profound because they are rarely discussed, let alone mastered. The level of quietude in your mind when the sensory input is consciously suspended offers tremendous peace of mind.

EXERCISE 6: THE WOMB POSE

One straightforward technique for finding this inner place of quietness is the Womb Pose. The image of the baby in the womb without use of its five senses is the archetype of this practice. Another helpful image is the turtle withdrawing its five limbs symbolically as each of the five senses are withdrawn. In this exercise, the five senses are symbolically closed. By consciously closing the five senses and ignoring any subtle sensations, the meditator is left alone with only internal thoughts as there are nearly no sensory stimuli to generate thoughts.

While sitting on the ground or in a comfortable seated posture, begin by placing the index fingers over the eyelashes (do not put pressure on the eyeball), the middle fingers on the bridge of the nose, the ring fingers above the lips, the smallest fingers (pinkies) below the lips and the thumbs gently over the ears. Then, hold the arms up parallel to the ground or lower the elbows. It is important to relax the hands so the arms remain relaxed. Also, it is recommended to prop the elbows on the knees if leaning against a back support. Do not permit any stiffness in your shoulder or neck area. Concentrate the mind at a point below the armpits, on the heart, or on the breathing. Practice from three to fifteen minutes, and as you do the exercise watch the mind slip to a place of inner tranquility—like in the womb. Come out of the practice slowly and notice how the senses influence the movements of the mind.

Developing Comfort with Silence

Are you comfortable with silence? From childhood, our lives have been guided by the lessons of surviving in the world. Having active senses and an active mind is part and parcel of being well adjusted. Sitting alone and eating in silence is not a culturally acceptable practice. In fact, silence is considered a punishment in childhood, and in many circles silence is viewed as being disconnected from others and even life itself.

On a deeper level, the human mind serves by thinking. Suddenly, meditation exercises are training the mind not to think, which could cause the mind to consider itself useless. What does a nonthinking mind do? If these questions are not considered thoroughly, the mind resists taking the next steps in its silence. In order to determine ways to overcome the active mind, see the following steps:

Summary of Steps for Quieting the Mind:

1. The mind is humanity's unique quality.

   The mind is an amazing feat of nature; not only can we communicate verbally but we can think, remember the past, and contemplate the future, as well as problem solve.

2. The mind is a helpful tool.

   The mind is nothing more than a tool, and like a tool it is to be used. We do not let the lawnmower drive us, do we?

3. The mind needs rest while awake.

   In order to improve or even maintain its optimal effectiveness, the mind needs renewal.

4. You are not only the thoughts of your mind.

Just as you are not only your physical body, you are much more than the thoughts of your mind.

5. Practice meditation to realize wisdom.

The mind calms with meditation and wisdom comes to recognize wisdom only from stillness.

Summary

As you begin to understand how your mind interprets information from your five senses, you may notice that no matter how hard you try, you just cannot accept a specific stimulus. The mind, for a valid reason, attaches a strong psychological connection to that stimulus. In these cases, you have to do some personal reflection to understand the basis for your mind's reactions. My beach memory example above demonstrates how my homesickness was very acute and my mind used a background sound as an excuse to daydream about home. The only way to gain harmony in my subsequent meditation would be to understand, accept, and honor the homesick feelings.

Most likely, you will feel that my example was very pleasant and even easy. You may feel that an annoying coworker or a difficult child may be much harder to quiet. You are most likely right; any situation we personally feel will always appear very difficult. In fact, it may seem impossible to solve the problem of a coworker yelling while on the telephone in the next cubicle. There are situations where behavior modifications may need to occur; in this case, the company may have to discipline the loud employee. However, the sentiment in your own mind may be examined and adjusted in each and every case of sensory stimulus you encounter. This is but one of the ways meditation transforms your life—there are a variety of stages before the mind fully quiets.

Part III
Six Types of Meditation

If you have been eager to start meditating, your time has arrived. Now that you have a clear set of objectives from part I, you are ready to commence or refine a lifelong journey of understanding your mind, your deepest self, and in so doing, reach your fullest potential. Part II of this book gave you tools to use on a daily basis prior to meditation practice to prepare you to focus. Part III introduces you to the six major types of meditation practices complete with theoretical summaries, meditation exercises, and feedback reflections. Be at ease with this process; one-hundred percent of students in our courses have easily determined their meditation type. You are much wiser when it comes to understanding your own mind.

Introduction to
Meditations for Your Type

Before each meditation type can be considered for its own qualities and benefits, a few words on the concept of meditation are warranted. Just as with any other pursuit of personal growth, from healthy diet to exercise, meditation requires daily practice. The foundational life-style approaches in part II for developing an environment favorable to meditation are only the beginning. With time and practice, meditation becomes a laboratory where you can make discoveries about your mind, personality, and deeper psyche. The more home practice you incorporate, the more time you spend in the laboratory and the more discoveries you will begin to make. Perhaps the greatest challenge to new meditators is finding time to dedicate to a consistent practice.

As this book is only intended as a means to finding the meditation style for your unique personality, what you ultimately do once you find it is up to you alone. If finding time to practice consistently is a major hurdle for beginners, then sticking with practice is the challenge for long-time meditators. It is well known among meditation teachers that belonging to a group is a powerful inspiration to keep home practice invigorating. It is also vital for the long-term maintenance of practice. As we begin to dive into the types of meditation, we refer you to the resources in part V which may be of assistance in finding local meditation groups, or at very least bringing your awareness to larger communities through web-based support organizations.

Cautions When Meditating

Meditation will not necessarily still the mind and bring inner peace right off the bat. The timing is unique for everyone and often unpredictable, but practice of meditation taps into everyone's psyche at a deep level. As the mind begins to quiet, deeper issues become exposed—just as the bottom of a lake becomes clearer as the ripples on the surface diminish. What lies beneath the surface is usually amplified in meditation; positive feelings of joy and peacefulness are much stronger, but difficult feelings of sadness or other pains may appear seemingly from nowhere and ambush the meditator who is seeking peace. While we must journey through the vicissitudes of life in our own way, expect that there may be emotional responses to meditation.

Another caution with emotions is in projecting those that occur unexpectedly. Projection of emotions means that someone applies or blames their personal inner state of mind on an unrelated subject, usually another person. If you find yourself having strong emotional reactions to close friends or family members (or others in your group should you begin practicing with one) it is our advice to seek the counsel of a meditation instructor for guidance.

The last sign of emotional overload we will address is the tendency to begin avoiding one's practice as intense issues arise. If the creatures swimming at the bottom of the lake are terrifying to behold, there is a natural fear to not wish to call them up again. However, the only way to overcome this fear and move past these deep issues is to bring them to the surface, bring them to light, and begin to understand their roots. Should you find yourself moving away from your practice due to one or more troubling insights, it is advised to again consult a meditation instructor. The most appropriate response may be as simple as journaling the emotion to slowly begin to process and understand it. Be careful not to think that meditation is the cause of these emotional states; meditation is merely the vehicle that navigates you through what is already in your mind.

One way to safeguard the self against these potential sways in emotion is to do one's best at staying balanced. It is fine to carry on laughing and crying; the balance comes in learning from the emotions that arise from the depths of the mind. Journaling and discussing what surfaces with trusted friends can be very healing exercises. Please be aware that there may be times where deep-seated, unresolved issues may arise which require the need for a professional counselor's aid to help bring closure and allow you to grow and move on. All things considered, meditation is without a doubt a practice for the brave!

How to Sit: Logistics

The term meditation may likely call to mind images of silent monks, sitting in perfect stillness atop their cushions. As I can attest from my first meditation experience in Japan, sitting on that cushion made my legs feel as though they had fallen off of my body—never had my legs been asleep for so long! "Sitting" in meditation is not just sitting, and it is important to understand how to sit and why. The greatest advice we can provide is to remember that if you feel any physical pain at all from sitting in meditation, you are completely allowed to reposition your body.

When it comes to the logistics of meditation, there are a few key principles to address. Perhaps the biggest is that while lying down may certainly appear to be the easiest way to bring stillness to the body, the reclining position is not suitable for meditation. It is without equal when it comes to relaxation, but in this position sleep will occur in almost everyone within eight to twelve minutes. As even brief meditation sessions should be at least fifteen minutes, this posture is simply not adequate. To thwart drowsiness, instead it is best to keep the spine fully erect, which positions the core upright, to allow maximal blood flow up into the brain to keep you awake. It may take some time to overcome any resistance to the muscles in the torso and core to keep you in a perfectly erect spine as much of our modern lifestyle consists of hunching forward at a desk or behind the wheel of a vehicle.

An added benefit of being upright in this manner is that it permits proper, natural breathing. It is amazing that even leaning forward slightly can compress the lungs and reduce breathing capacity. From this straight spine, it is encouraged to bring a slight smile or half-grin to the face, which can help relax the body, settle the shoulders and neck, and even calm the mind. With the upper body in a comfortable, happy place, you can then begin to direct your attention to the lower half.

Unlike in my initial meditation experience, the key is keeping the legs as comfortable as possible; even sitting in a chair is perfectly acceptable if being on the ground is painful. Contrary to some teachings and styles, pain is to be avoided in meditation as it draws your focus away from the real intention. In terms of pain, it is not only the legs that can become uncomfortable in seated meditation; the tailbone and coccyx (base of the spine) can actually compress inwards if sitting improperly, yielding discomfort. Keeping the pelvis tilted slightly forward helps alleviate the final area of potential pain in meditation, the low back. A forward-tilt of the pelvis encourages the skeleton to support the upper body. Letting the pelvis tip backwards rounds the low back and forces those muscles to support the torso, which leads to backaches in very short order. If you cannot keep the back from rounding on a cushion, then sitting in a chair is a perfectly acceptable posture for meditation.

While the "traditional" meditation is with the legs crossed in the seated position, the ultimate idea is of stillness and acceptance of your own unique situation. Having the legs bent into a butterfly position, or opened into a wide "V" are also fine practice positions. It is strongly recommended to vary your posture from time to time so that the body does not become strained from sitting in one position all the time. Finally, if you are comfortable on a cushion, it is best to sit as close to the front edge as possible so that the legs can rest entirely on the ground in front of you. Sitting way back on the cushion can actually cause the front edge to press the underside of the thighs and decrease circulation to the legs, ultimately resulting in pain. Just remember that the knees and low back are the two areas that can be strained in prolonged seated meditation. Be mindful of how they feel and know it is just fine to practice from a comfortable chair!

To conclude this introduction to the formal meditation techniques to follow in the next few chapters, we refer you back to chapter 6 for a short, nonexhaustive list of suitable postures for meditation practice.

Feel free to experiment with these in each of the different types of meditation. Perhaps a particular combination will resonate strongly with you.

Time to Enter the Meditation Laboratory

As I mentioned in the introduction, even with twenty years experience as a meditation teacher, predicting a person's meditation style is elusive. Psychologists do not have an assessment form to prescribe the ultimate meditation style—I have already tried to devise my own form to no avail. The only solution is old-fashioned trial and error. Please give this book—a version of our successful meditation course—some time and effort. You will discover that one or two meditation types will take you to a deeper quietude than other types.

In this case, the advice is to take the path of least resistance and use the meditation style that offers maximum focus to your mind.

Meditation Experiment Summaries

At the conclusion of each of the chapters in part III (one each on the different methods of meditation) there is a set of summary questions for you to consider after dabbling in the various exercises in the book. Remember that these conclusions are just for you to begin to reflect on your personal affinities regarding which type or types of meditation are best suited to calm your mind. Use your own scale to compare and contrast. While I have been unable to predict results for students and unable to make a psychological test (it would have been much easier than writing an entire book!), I have found that hundreds of students have figured their type out easily on their own.

Happy meditating!

Ten
....

Type 1: Breath

Absolute statements can only be made about a very few things, and breathing is one of those things. Absolutely, you will die if you go four minutes without breathing. Absolutely, every religious tradition on the planet refers to breath. Every martial art, natural healing art, and yoga tradition values breathing. Every form of medicine on the planet observes breathing. Breathing is part and parcel the most fundamental aspect of anyone's life. As this is more of a handbook than a historical book, I encourage you to please do the research; every meditation group also discusses the breath. Despite all of this, however, only a portion of the population will find these types of more somatic-based meditation exercises a fit. Let us see if it is for you!

Breath Awareness

Of all the systems in the body, respiration is the only one that is both subconsciously and consciously controlled. The breath and the mind are intimately connected, and the ancient yogis used to teach that the breath is a bridge between the realm of the mind and that of the physical body. Meditation on the breath takes this fundamental link to facilitate a steadier mind and body. Recall back to the chapter in part II on deep breathing: how do you find yourself feeling when your breath is short and shallow as opposed to slow and deep? When we are anxious or upset, the mind takes control of the breathing pattern to our detriment. As we discussed, the alternative is also true: if we allow our breath to come short and rapid, the state of our minds will become agitated.

EXERCISE 1: UNSTRUCTURED AWARENESS ON THE BREATH

The first exercise for meditating on the breath is to simply let yourself breathe and observe how your mind follows and reacts to your breath. It is not the intention of this exercise to control either the breath or what the mind is doing, simply to witness what occurs in your mind with a natural breath. As this awareness begins to build, you may experiment with controlling the breath to different degrees—making it faster or slower, deeper, or shallower—and again just observing how the mind reacts. Throughout these exercises, also observe your feelings.

- Do you feel energy moving with the breath into and out of the body, circulating with the natural rhythm?

- Do you visualize light or colors in your body with the influx of each fresh breath? Or maybe the inhalation inspires feelings of emptiness, as if you are becoming the incorporeal breath.

- Does a familiar prayer come to mind, or do you find yourself in deep conversation with a divine being or cosmic manifestation?

What you feel in this simple exercise is a major clue into the meditation for your unique type. Notice how you feel after two minutes, then at ten minutes, and if you sit longer, at twenty minutes. The mind may take a certain amount of time so settle into the exercise.

This seemingly simple practice is in fact critical for preparing your mind for deeper meditation down the road. As Swami Rama explains in his book *Science of Breath*, the mind's tendency is to identify itself with things in the material realm. If the mind is scattered without, it will never be able to focus and start looking inward. Reassociation of the mind's focus, the swami says, is initiated by a smooth, steady, and even breath. With this breath, there is little cause for mental distraction. When the breath is erratic and choppy, or coming in gasps, it comes as no surprise that the mind is easily disrupted, for sound and physical motion draw the mind away from the inner state.

Exercise 2: Focusing on the Throat

One such exercise for breath awareness is focusing on the windpipe or the top of the bronchial tubes in the throat. Bringing focus to this region of the body is taught to yield calmness of mind. This is a traditional practice and is quite profound in its simplicity. The *Yoga Sutras* instruct us to observe the breath passing in and out of the throat area (III.31). Find a comfortable seated position, close your eyes, place the hands folded near the navel and begin to concentrate on the breath coming from this navel area. By simply witnessing the breath move in and out, the mind remains still and kept under focus. It is important to resist the temptation to actually follow the air as it passes through the throat down into the lungs; you are not becoming the air in this exercise. As you might expect, the mind must be active to trace the route of the air flow and an active mind can be distracted in such manner. This practice hopes to mimic a still mind which, like a bird, simply perches and observes from a vantage point. An important thing to consider is that swallowing is also a distraction. In this (and most other) practices, it is strongly encouraged to gently place the tip of the tongue at the top of the mouth. Though saliva will still build up, its production will slow greatly.

As you continue to focus on the top area of the throat, allow the concentration to be passive, still, and stable. From this single point, it can be helpful to recognize and contemplate how life revolves on its endless pulse. Though the conscious mind has its own perspectives, the heart continues to beat and thus the mind is ultimately not responsible for life, merely intimately connected to it. When overly active, the mind disrupts this natural process by attempting to direct and control the outcomes of life. Life is going to take its course smoothly and in its own way. When the mind understands this, its proper role in serving life is emphasized instead of trying to control the uncontrollable.

Focusing on the breath slowly begins to still the mind, and as the mind stills even deeper levels of the subconscious can be explored. Thus awareness of breath really is the gateway into more subtle meditation practices. Breathing allows the mind to focus its energy to a single, discrete point, and much like a laser is a concentrated beam of light, the intensity of the mind's focus is enhanced the more one-pointed it becomes. While many meditation exercises use breathing as an auxiliary prop, honing one's practice of breath awareness alone will allow much deeper experiences as you progress on your meditation journey.

One thing that novice and regular meditatiors notice quite quickly during these breath awareness exercises is that it is not easy to keep the mind focused on the breath! For even a mind with some meditation training, witnessing the breath is not sustainable—the mind invariably begins to drift. Fortunately the *Yoga Sutras* provide a safeguard: contemplating the meaning of breath in a spiritual way, for without such a spiritual intention the mind grows restless in short order (II.49). Like the example above about life going on without the mind's conscious control, see if you can couple your individual experience of breathing with a deeper meaning. Breathing can certainly equal life and existence, but also gratitude, love, or compassion. Take the time to examine your personal intention for meditation, as it is likely perfect to use for the deeper meaning of breathing.

Chakras and Energetic Flow

In the classical yogic philosophy, human existence is subdivided into five bodies or sheaths, called the *koshas*. Like concentric circles, these sheaths contain and affect the others. The outermost sheath is the physical body, linked to food. In closest contact to our physical beings is the sheath of *prana*—a term in yoga used to mean breath, life force, and vital energy. Breath and energy are intertwined, as evidenced when we are undergoing vigorous exercise and become short of breath; endurance tends to wane as we struggle to breathe deeply. Alternatively, when the breath comes deeply and smoothly, feelings of circulating energy can be felt as the systems of the body work more efficiently.

The ancient yogis characterized this energetic system into seven psycho-spiritual centers known as *chakras*. Located along the path of the spine, from the base of the tailbone to the crown of the head, each chakra possesses its own aspects of nature, personality, elements, and anatomical domains. Before introducing the chakra system and the role of the breath, first consider what it feels like to have "energy" in the body. A fine example is how loving interactions can create a feeling of warmth in the area of the heart. The experience of love, a very spiritual thing, has a somatic response and that response is localized to a particular area of the body. Just as tensions may settle in the body, positive experiences can vibrate the chakra centers in healthy ways. Other examples of common psychosomatic experiences are feeling "butterflies in the stomach" before making a big speech or performance and a sensation in the center of the forehead during deep thinking or contemplation.

Exercise 3: Understanding Energetic Feelings
Consider a time when you can vividly recall having felt energy in the body. Ask yourself the series of following questions to begin to gain understanding of the feeling of energy moving and working in your body.

- What is the property of the energy you feel? Is it warm, cold, hot, moist, or dry?

- Is there a color or colors associated with the feeling of energy? Was it intense and focused in a particular area or more diffuse in brightness and location?

- Was there a strong emotion manifesting at the time? Did that emotion have effects on any part of the body?

- Did a sound, a particular song, or some other tune come to mind during the feeling of energy? Do you have any insights into your relationship to that audible expression?

- Could you detect the movement of the energy in a particular direction like swirling, vibrating, or circulating?

Probing your energetic experiences with these types of questions may help you begin to understand the reality of the chakras in your physical body as well as assist you in increasing your overall perception and awareness.

Exercise 4: Chakras—The Energy "Wheels"

Energy and breath intertwine in the body as the energy connects and channels the breath into the chakra points. Both the breath and the chakras themselves are expressions of life-force energy (*prana*) in the mind-body system. For some, aligning the breath with a specific area of the body can be a powerful practice of meditation. The concept behind the process is quite simple: the breath acts to charge up the chakra area. As the breath charges the chakra energetically like a battery, the mind remains fixed in concentration on the concepts embodied by that chakra, thus associating a significant meaning for meditation. Table 1 below outlines the names and some of the elements embodied by the chakras, with colors indicating a common representation of each, while Figure 1 illustrates their commonly accepted physical location within the body. If chakras and the energy body are of special interest to you, please refer to our reference section for further materials to expand your knowledge and understanding.

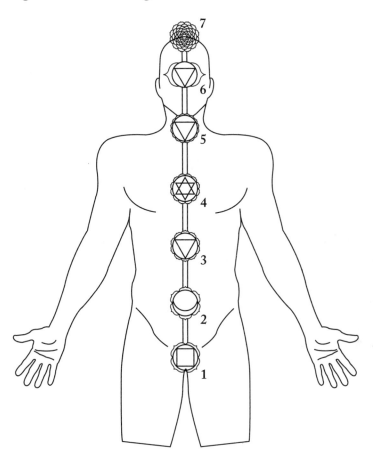

Figure 1: Physical representation of the chakras in the body. Numbers correspond to those in Table 1.

TABLE 1: COMMON ELEMENTS EMBODIED BY THE CHAKRAS

Number	Sanskrit Name	Common Name	Elements
1	Muladhara	Root Chakra	Family, groundedness, and sustainability
2	Svadisthana	Water Chakra	Emotion, creative energy, and spontaneity
3	Manipura	Fire Chakra	Digestion, willpower, and self-esteem
4	Anahata	Heart Chakra	Love, compassion, and giving and receiving
5	Vishuddha	Purity Wheel	Communication between heart and mind
6	Ajna	Third Eye	Vision, wisdom, and clarity
7	Sahasrara	Crown Chakra	Spirituality, beliefs, and universal connectedness

If meditating on a chakra center resonates with you, all you really have to do is focus your mind and intention on that chakra. You must be careful, however, not to turn the meditation into a moving exercise where you jump from one chakra to the next! Simply observe one area and apply the meaning of that chakra as you feel it as an aspect of your intention.

Next, you can connect the breath to the chakra. As you concentrate on the chakra, you will effectively use the mind to charge that energy center. Imagine you are breathing energy into the chakra and see it fill as your lungs expand. In some cases, you may actually feel warmth or a tingling feeling in the corresponding area of the body. Have fun with it, and allow your own personality to determine the sensory experience, not shaping it in any way. Some common senses are visions or seeing colored light, sensations of touch, feeling warmth, detecting a soft sound, or "hearing" the meaning of the chakra repeated over and over.

EXERCISE 5: LIGHTENING UP!—SMILE BREATH MEDITATION

An old saying goes that "laughter is the best medicine" and many recent medical reports seem to show evidence of it. Whole yoga classes are dedicated to "laughter yoga" where audible sounds akin to laughter are made in tandem with the postures or simply just pure laughter. Ultimately, these classes culminate with everyone hilariously giggling! Many yoga and meditation programs fall into the pitfall of being far too serious, when in fact unencumbered joy actually promotes a focused mind. Though meditation aims to uncover the complexities of the mind by moving towards the often difficult meditative state, it does not mean that the lighthearted attitude must disappear. Blending dedication to disciplined practice and the openness of levity is a solid recipe for long term success in meditation.

In Taoist literature, this light approach is known as Inner Smile Meditation. Before moving within, the practice begins by sitting comfortably like any other meditation practice with the spine erect, but then making a full, huge grin on your face. As you breathe naturally, begin to feel the sensations of the muscles needed to smile, especially in the cheeks and eyes. Progressing into meditation, the smile begins to fade into a gentle grin; however the cheeks and eyes remain in a position that reflects positivism. In this practice the smile represents vitality and life itself, brought on by feeling strong in the body and mind. Children blessed with good health and emotional support smile most of the time. This universal expression harbors tremendous power and can be a gripping meditation technique.

Once the grin has been established and the sensations of the muscles committed to conscious awareness, the process of smiling meditation occurs in two steps. First, the visual image of the smile on your face gets moved and circulated to every part of the body, facilitated by the breath. Feel the smiling vitality and life-force energy on your face, then beneath your face into your brain and nervous system. Breathe the smiling energy deep into your lungs and let the breath carry the smile to your muscles, bones, tendons, and visceral organs. Enjoy the entire "smile body scan" as you prepare the mind and body to become more open to receiving positive energy.

The second step requires concentration on the smile itself and using that gentle smile to charge the air that you breathe in. Continue to meditate on this image of the smile and breath being the deliverers of this positive energy into the body for the duration of your practice. As thoughts or disturbances arise, you can greet them with the gentle, compassionate smile and let them simply drift away. The grin or half-smile you establish in this practice can be incorporated as your normal facial expression; something Buddhist monk and experienced meditator Thich Nhat Hahn emphasises greatly. When greeting others, waiting in a line, sitting on the bus, at work, or doing chores around the house, allow your default facial expression to be a soft, positive half-smile. You may be surprised at the internal results and the responses from those around you!

Breath Meditation
Experiment Summary

The questions below are repeated at the end of each of the meditation exercise chapters of part III. Recognize that the responses are relative to your experience. You can create your own method of comparing and contrasting the exercises. Also, make adjustments for the fact that when you practice after a busy day (compared to a relaxing Sunday), your mind will be in a different state. The ultimate goal is to settle on one practice, but at this point, dabbling is fine. By the conclusion of the book, you will have the tools and experiences to establish one meditation method and stick with that for a longer period of months or years.

Summary

Each type-specific chapter is merely a summary of a much more involved meditation path. After practicing as suggested in this chapter, take a pause for reflection and answer the following questions.

1. What stood out as significant for you in this chapter's practices?

2. Do you have any insight about why these were important for you? Do they relate to habitual patterns?

3. Note any other reasons why that certain exercise resonated with you.

4. Did this exercise help you becoming more aware of the interplay of thoughts and emotions?

5. What exercise felt right?

Use your intuition or gut reaction to this. Try to remove preconceived notions of which exercise you "should" practice or which exercise you may have tried earlier in your life.

Eleven

Type 2: Affirmations and Visualization

In some form or another, we all have had experiences with visualization—either positively or negatively. "Psyching up" before an athletic event or performance, where you see yourself excelling at the task ahead is a form of imagining the goal in your mind and then applying effort towards that outcome. On the other hand, it is entirely possible to "psyche out" before an equally intense event!

Visualization is an ancient practice, originating to the earliest spiritual traditions. Even before that, from the times of the earliest artists, those Neolithic cave painters, the concept of visualizing has existed in the human mind. These cave painters had to first envision meaningful aspects of their lives, and from these thoughts they were able to create sometimes even more meaningful symbols and pictures. The images, as crude as we may think them now, filled the minds of these cave dwellers and directed them for survival and ultimately inner peace along the way.

Understanding
Visualization Conceptually

To be clear, visualization includes using imagination, the mind's eye, and imagery as outward techniques. However, with all meditation techniques, there is also an internal aspect that relates to the intention for the meditation practice. Visualization focuses directly on one's beliefs system to create affirmations for the various visual exercises.

Visualization originated with ancient spiritual traditions. Inherent in many of these traditions is the belief that a force larger than one's self controls reality. Our wishes are typically shortsighted and not far reaching and may not always serve the greatest good. For one, we humans may not be able to comprehend and understand even the littlest workings of nature, let alone the absolutes. There is a thin line between life and death, the vibrantly healthy person suddenly stricken with disease or the unpredictable accident when everything else is going "right." Sometimes an illness is actually a lesson and blessing in disguise to teach someone the value of good health and wellness. A terrible addiction may transform someone during the recovery phase, opening that person to insights and ways of living he or she never would have experienced before. In order to visualize with the greatest good in mind, it helps to remove our expectations first.

Though some nonsecular authors have been able to capture this essence, it is very difficult to explain non-attachment and remain secular. When one utilizes visualization to succeed, the idea of nonattachment seems almost contrary to the achievement of the goal. If the athlete wants to win the race, she is aware of the time she must beat; if the businessman has to sell twenty accounts, his paycheck will depend on his sales. The common response is to visualize the goal of the winning time or the highest number of sales. However, the problem with these "success"-driven uses of visualization lie in the focus on quantity, not quality; this external type of thinking focuses on results, material goals, and desired ends.

To begin to unravel the conundrum of goals, results, and visualization, an emphasis on virtuous behavior can lead visualization to its intended end while remaining morally upright and nonattached. The athlete seeking inner peace and lasting happiness from her sport can attempt to reach her greatest potential while running. Each stride may be fluid, focused, and powerful. The discipline and sacrifice of daily training may increase her humility. If this athlete improves herself as a person while training and running towards her highest potential, she wins every race as her goal extends beyond the physical distance. As a side benefit, if she reaches her potential, she will be fast! A good affirmation to for this athlete is "I am reaching my full potential by running" (more on affirmations a bit later in this chapter). The businessman may think in terms of being ethical, hardworking, creative, and successful. His affirmation could be "I am remaining centered while I creatively sell the accounts." Such focused individuals act in a manner that achieves greatness as a side effect of remaining focused in the living moment.

In *Creative Visualization*, Shakti Gawain offers a powerful quote that remains secular and unattached: "This, or something better, now manifests for me in totally satisfying and harmonious ways for the highest good of all concerned" (Gawain, 1978, 33). This type of thinking is important in the case of visualizing for achievement. Likewise, when visualizing for some specific result one does not control (like most everything!), a sense of failure may occur at some point. A humble attitude on non-attachment ensures that the visualization serves a virtuous purpose regardless of the outcome or our wishes for it.

On Awareness

Before one can begin to use visualizations positively, one must first make healthy affirmations to one's self. An iceberg reveals only its tip above the water, the majority of it hides below the surface. Most of our consciousness complex—memories, knowledge, thought patterns—is like the iceberg, residing below the surface of our awareness. One of the first steps in visualizing anything is being able to relate to the unconscious mind. As our deeper thought patterns are understood, replacing the old pattern with a positive intention is very effective. The difficulty or near impossibility of knowing the unconsciousness makes the task of "knowing ourselves" a lifelong puzzle to piece together. By simply focusing on a positive image in relationship to our health we may begin to uncover our previously unconscious viewpoint.

No matter how much we practice, most of us have some weaknesses in our personalities; for example, varying degrees of low self-esteem are common. We may intellectually understand and comprehend the meaning of meditation but remain unable to practice. For example, most of us are well aware that junk food, sweets, cigarettes, and alcohol are detrimental to good health, yet our culture consumes vast quantities of soda, cigarettes, and alcohol. The reasons for continuing with unhealthy living habits such as addictions, fear, laziness, attachment to pleasures, (amongst others) could fill volumes. When you work on visualizing positively, try to bring awareness to any negative tendencies you discover. These tendencies at the core level will reside in beliefs that are stored in the unconscious. These beliefs are not necessarily rational. This next exercise aims at understanding the essence of limiting attitudes with the goal of transforming these deeply held beliefs.

Exercise 1: Name Your Family of Origin's Top Ten Beliefs
(and notice how similar yours are to them)
Please be aware of—and compassionate to—the fact that even if you do not agree with some or many aspects of your family of origin, your

unconscious most likely shares many beliefs of your extended family to a large degree. For example, I once heard a friend speak of the power of sit-ins. He wanted a group of graduate students to protest the Gulf War at a time when no one else was protesting. He wanted us to fast and overtake the chapel at the university. His views were very accurate, but the tone itself was overzealous. Not long thereafter, I met the man's parents and spoke to his father at some length. Once his father became comfortable with me, out of the blue he asked, "You seem like a nice boy. Do you believe in the power of Jesus Christ?" That same overenthusiasm of the son's sit-in came from the father. Mind you, the son had long ago rebelled against "the Church and the entire establishment" as he would put it, but the same zeal remained with both father and son.

Over the years, I have tested this theory with meditation students and found that just as people hold belief systems, families too share common beliefs. I have witnessed profound shifts when a person is able to understand his or her family of origin's beliefs. When the child in the dynamic rejects the family's beliefs, the same beliefs appear with a different outward appearance—like above, zealous conservative father, zealous liberal son. Once these beliefs are understood, they can be accepted. Once accepted, they can be honored. This is a difficult thing to ask of you, and it may initiate a longer-term process. It is, however, a key to free your mind in the process of self-realization. If this exercise holds power for you, it is a sign that visualization could be a good practice for you.

1. Write down the core beliefs of your family of origin. Include beliefs that may be shared by the community where you were raised. Please list what you would say are the top ten beliefs held by your family system. To discover underlying beliefs, think of behaviors that your family holds as ritual and inquire as to the reasons why until you reach the underlying belief.

For example, as a child, Joe's parents visited the grandparents every week. They gave the grandparents attention and handled any affairs needed. Belief: the family believes in serving elders and in general, serving those in need. In contrast to this example, Joe's parents always complained about how little other relatives did for the grandparents. But in front of the relatives, Joe's parents would be helpful and not say a word. Belief: Joe's parents believe in keeping the peace at all costs but permit venting in private.

2. Examine how you either practice the above beliefs like your family or how you have adapted those same beliefs and practice something else.

3. If you resent or resist any of your family of origins beliefs (or more bluntly, strongly abhor the family's beliefs) try to first forgive them for being that way and then begin to examine how you are repeating that pattern.

Until you are able to accept others within yourself, you are most likely repeating the issue.

At this point, you may be wondering how this exercise is related to finding the meditation for your type. Visualization is one type of practice that happens to be very powerful at transforming deeply held beliefs.

Developing Affirmations

"Self-talk" is another thing to ward against when beginning to visualize and work through your affirmations. Like a quiet echo, this mental chatter may repeat thoughts and ideas unconsciously in your mind. Positive as well as negative memories and future projections float around in our minds. Before a speech, for example, the rookie's mind may chatter: "What if I make a mistake? What if I forget something?" The veteran presenter, however, visualizes in a positive manner—delivering an eloquent speech—and repeats as an affirmation: "Let us have a fruitful lecture." Some of the key concepts to keep in mind for affirmations are as follows:

1. Accept negative self-talk without worry.

   Resisting negativity creates fear and more negativity. After accepting the negative facet, change it in that living moment. For example: "I am a bad mother because I burned supper!" Instead, accept yourself and the events that transgressed and say them aloud: "Dinner was burned because I was changing my baby's diaper and forgot to turn off the stove." In fact, you were not a bad mother at all, but were caring for your child's immediate needs. You can then affirm yourself that "I am a devoted mother. Now, what can we eat?" In this acceptance of what is, the situation transforms. As you discover your affirmation, cultivate it daily.

2. Take the time to write your affirmation with ONLY positive images.

   The statement "I am no longer an inexperienced parent" creates first the image of a bad parent. Our minds can rationalize negative and positive concepts, but images are much more charged and clear. Affirming instead that "I am a caring parent" helps to shift the mind's visual imagery towards more positive states.

3. Use the present tense.

   We exist in the living moment of the present. What happened a few moments ago or what will happen in short order are not the here and now. Statements like "I will become…" or "I am trying to…" have a weak tone to them, do not create an immediate image and are not of the present moment. The present tense affirmation describes the positive image in your mind at this very moment; not yesterday and not tomorrow. Avoid other types of temporal statements like "I am a smart person except when I am tired" or "I am at peace, but not if I do not meditate daily." See if you can frame it to be more encompassing and positive: "I am intelligent, and because I am smart I rest when I am tired," or

"Meditating daily supports inner peace and I am at peace as I accept the changing reality called life."

4. Be short and simple.

Avoid complex or long-winded affirmations; you should be able to remember the phrase at any time! In addition to staying simple, it should also be unique to you as it is your affirmation. Try to make the affirmation fresh and alive by creating it entirely yourself. It can help to relate the affirmation to your current life situations as well.

5. Believe in yourself (and your affirmation).

As was hinted at in the previous section, you are what you believe and what you perceive. Faith is a powerful ally in overcoming negative tendencies and moving towards more positive, healthy ways of approaching the world. Affirming yourself as "the best" of something relies on an ultimately near impossible perfection that will likely be hard to believe or have faith in. However, reaching for your highest potential is entirely believable.

Exercise 2: Creating Your Affirmation

Utilizing the five steps for building an affirmation, begin to form a corresponding affirmation for a positive image on which you do or wish to meditate. Remember to formulate the "goal" in accordance with growth of virtue and nonattachment. Take your time and have fun with this exercise, making the affirmation as unique as your own personality. Think of the quality of feeling that you will gain if your goal was reached. For example, if I want to be married and have a family, the resultant feeling would be living in a loving dynamic. The way to remove obstacles in your deeper mind is to hold onto that feeling by using the virtue that represents that feeling. The focus on "love" will allow the deeper need to be resolved. From this deeper perspective, your mind will feel more at peace. The tendency to be needy that blocks the ultimate goal fades as you focus on what you need in the moment. If you have a family, you know that even in a dynamic that may appear loving, you still need to focus on how to love from the inside. You can come back to this exercise any time new challenges or situations arise in your life.

Below are examples of affirmations demonstrated from the perspective of a goal morphed into a freeing statement. Make sure to personalize your affirmation and use the list below only as a guide.

Goal:	Affirmation:
Get married and have a family.	Love fills my heart.
Find a job.	I am a productive person.
Better relationship with my brother.	I accept my brother, unconditionally.
Improve health.	I am vital and full of energy.
Lose weight.	I am supported.
Lose weight.	I appreciate my life as it is.
Lose weight.	My body is full of light.

Notice that the final three examples begin with the same goal of losing weight. However, the affirmations are completely different. This example may help you realize that the ultimate goal is an inner state of mind.

How to Visualize

This applied question can be answered by a short, simple visual exercise. After you read this sentence, close your eyes and imagine your bedroom, and without any other instructions, observe how you handle this simple task.

�֍

How was that brief experience? Were you able to see the room in your mind like a photograph? Did you "know" the relationship of your bed to other objects and how the dresser is so many steps from the door? Perhaps you visualized the room in terms of broader space and the feeling of the room itself? Did you invoke your memory and imagination when recalling your bedroom? Were you able to think about the room as a means of visualizing, or did you simply see things as they were in the room? While there may not be many other possibilities, if one of these responses did not resonate with your personal experience, take a moment to journal your unique method of visualization.

We all visualize or associate images with thoughts, so we already know how to unconsciously visualize. However, it may be difficult at first to place the new images in your mind. In the case that visualization is indeed foreign, you will want to give yourself the time to learn your own method. Following the "right way" of visualizing (or the "right way" of many other skills) may cause you to practice a mental exercise foreign to your own unique way of thinking. Hence the little experience above, to bring you into deeper awareness of how your mind formulates images. As you begin to learn how you visualize, you only add to your abilities.

EXERCISE 3: RESHAPE YOURSELF

As part of human nature, we often see things archetypically. Certain images or characteristics evoke deep-seated thoughts or responses. These archetypes can be powerful symbols. Archetypes come in many varieties on a cultural scale, but we also archetype ourselves. In a comfortable seated position, close your eyes and begin to imagine or visualize how you personally see yourself. Be as creative and exaggerated as you would like. Try to be very honest. As you develop and paint this internal image of yourself, begin to notice the flaws in the painting—don't be critical—but be objective and accepting.

Next, see if you can look at the picture and instead of being tempted to alter or delete what you see, try to replace the area of weakness and reshape it with an uplifting framework. If you see an insecure person in a business suit, try instead to reshape it to see the same person in the same suit standing up straight and tall with a nice smile on his or her face. Or, if you see a body that is out of shape, then visualize that same body glowing with vibrant health and making healthful choices.

Visualizing for health is probably the most common underlying thread for many practitioners. When you visualize vital health, the aim is to attempt to reach deeper levels of your unconscious. As you make affirmations of good health behaviors, make sure that you intentionally nurture your existing disciplines. Most people eat some whole foods, care for their teeth and skin, take time daily for rest, exercises to some degree, study health literature, and breathe deeply during the day. Feeling inadequacy over "all" the good behaviors you *could* be doing makes change feel overwhelming. Truth be told, no one could physically do everything good for their health all of the time; there are just not enough hours in the day. The key is to remain positive when you visualize for health by remembering the good things you *do* practice as you work towards making your visualization reality.

This example can certainly be applied to any other theme of affirmation. Staying with this theme, when you do visualize good health, remember the five steps to building an affirmation: short and simple, positive, believable, present, and unique. The following are some classic affirmations which may provide you inspiration (remember, your affirmation needs to be our own personal expression!):

- "My spirit's vitality fills my body."

- "Deep breath brings vital energy through me."

- "I am practicing a healthy lifestyle."

Once these positive ideas are repeated in your mind, you may begin to view healthy behaviors as normal. Eating well no longer becomes a task—you know no other way to eat. As positive health images gain momentum, you will be more likely to find ways to maintain a positive viewpoint. In other words, you start to think more and more like the person living the healthy lifestyle you are visualizing. You would naturally tend to exercise regularly, eat well, rest sufficiently, practice yoga and meditation daily, and perform any other personal practices that add to your positive self image.

Meditation with Visualization

Now that we have discussed what visualization is, how to construct affirmations as a means to visualization and how to actually visualize, we proceed to utilizing visualization as a meditation practice. In reality, the daily affirmations and visualization practices you perform are minimeditations with a less fully focused mind. The formal meditation with visualization removes any other distractions from daily living and allows full concentration on the image you have chosen to create.

Exercise 4: Visualizing Vitality

Find yourself a comfortable meditative posture, close your eyes and begin to let the breathing settle and slow. Focus your mind on radiant health with an image or affirmation that you have created to fit your unique self. Use your own method to create this healthy visualization (from the "How to Visualize" section). Follow the standard pattern of a healthy, vital spirit within your body. However, since the body is not under one's complete control, begin to shift your focus on the mind. Remember that you may be healthy in mind and spirit no matter how the body is doing. The ninety-year-old person with a youthful vigor and frail frame may be healthier than the overstressed, mentally extinguished middle-aged workaholic who is moderately physically fit. Sit with the image of vibrant health for the duration of your practice. This is a fantastic exercise to practice daily before retiring to sleep.

In the beginning, visualization images are fixed and you imagine concretely. To be relaxed while driving, for example, you focus on visualizing a deep-breathing, relaxed driver. When meditating with visualization for a longer period of time and with more experience, you may become more receptive in your approach. The receptive or passive mode allows images to form or pass through the mind more fluidly, so long as the images remain related to your meditation topic. If the mind does wander (which it may), return yourself to the original, concrete image. The receptive mode of meditating may help you when processing a problem or seeking an insight through visualization as the mind is more open to possibilities instead of adhering to a single focus.

Blocks to Visualization

Visualization may seem quite natural, for recall it has been a part of our collective heritage for thousands of years. Despite this, visualization is not always so easy. Take a moment to consider the blocks to visualization as your mind may have the natural disposition to visualize but factors in your experience could be interfering with your natural ability. Remember one of the main themes of this book is using the methods that are most natural for quieting your mind versus trying what does not work.

Depending on the nature of a situation or a memory of past situations, mental barriers may form around certain images, preventing moving towards making a visualization reality. The psycho-spiritual term "block" relates to any aspect of one's personality that acts as a barricade to stop all traffic in your mind. You may try and try to overcome an issue from low self-esteem to forgiveness only to meet a mental brick wall. No matter how hard you try to change or how determined your practice is, nothing happens; discipline eludes you and good intentions remain the stuff of imagination.

The extreme roadblock to visualization is a trauma you witnessed firsthand. Due to the shock of visual trauma, when you attempt to visualize, your mind may tend to seize and go blank. This sort of block indicates unresolved emotions that have yet to be acknowledged. Such extreme blocks may require professional assistance, and that is perfectly acceptable. Less difficult negative emotions may cause a similar resistance to meditation or personal growth, and these are the ones that we can personally work at. These "lesser" blocks leave us missing one specific quality and cause us to find any excuse to not further activities for our growth. Ultimately, these unresolved issues lead to bigger problems. Focusing your mind on a positive visualization may help you to confront the weaknesses. Listed below are a few examples I have seen in my time teaching people these practices, and alternative affirmations that can bring freedom. You will notice that not all of these may appear negative on the surface!

Block	Freedom
No pain, no gain	Consciousness expansion is bliss
Pain is the only motivator	Daily spiritual practice is a way of life
I am a lowly sinner	I am a child of God
Caring for others means self-sacrifice	Caring for others empowers you
Poverty is holy	Living simply is freedom

I do not wish to be better than others

I live to my fullest potential to bless all

I fear being true to myself

I take small, courageous steps forward

I worry incessantly about things

I pray for concerns dear to my heart

My life is too busy for meditation

I prioritize self-care

The steps to overcome blocks and start moving toward freedom begin with honestly confronting and identifying the block. Come face to face with the wall in your mind and critically examine it. See if you can give a name to the emotions and thought patterns you are observing in this block. The writing is on the wall, so to speak; so read thoroughly! Once you have identified your barrier, begin to search for its roots. A wall is only as good as its foundations, so seek out the base, tracing back the emotions or thought patterns to the vital essence of the block. When you have the cause, you may attempt either individually or with the assistance of others to attempt to heal the block. Self-analysis, honesty, and compassion are the main tools to begin to take down the wall. As you begin to chip away at the block with your introspection, use your affirmations and other practices to channel healthy, positive energy to embolden and strengthen your personality. As your strength grows, the block becomes little more than a speed bump, and as you continue to work on the issue with full acceptance, the barrier is little more than a memory.

Continuing with Visualization

In this chapter we have used visualization and affirmation in and out of meditation practice for better living. If this type of practice resonates with you, we encourage you to carry it forward to continue the benefits of visualization over time by continuing and maintaining a positive focus. Try to create a habit of visualizing by posting your current visualization topic on your refrigerator, in the car, at your desk at work, and in the bathroom or your bedroom. As you use visualization, you will find that it is good to change the topic every few months to suit the needs of your present life situation. In time, maintaining a positive image becomes a habit. The mental chatter and self-talk may still be there, but you may find that they slowly begin to change their tune to more positive notes!

You may also wish to experiment and expand the way that you visualize. Recall from the exercise on imagining your bedroom that there are many qualities that represent different aspects of visualization, such as: feeling, mood, pictures, space, memory, imagination, and color. You can try to remember the positive feeling of the visual image. You may sense the emotional mood that you gain from the image. Maybe you picture yourself in the setting with a clear state of mind. Or perhaps you are more aware of the space around you in the image. Try memorizing the image—make it a catchy rhyme or jingle that you could hum or sing! Be creative and remain open to your imagination as you expand your positivity. You could also experience the image in vibrant, living color. And remember, you can have positive images and affirmations for all the areas of your life, such as work, relaxation, intimate relationships, health, meditation, diet, exercise, and so on.

Summary

Each type-specific chapter in this book is merely a summary of a much more involved meditation path. After practicing as suggested in this chapter, take a pause for reflection and answer the following questions.

1. What stood out as significant for you in this chapter's practices?

2. Do you have any insight about why these were important for you? Do they relate to habitual patterns?

3. Note any other reasons why that certain exercise resonated with you.

4. Did this exercise help you becoming more aware of the interplay of thoughts and emotions?

5. What exercise felt right?

Use your intuition or gut reaction to this. Try to remove precon-ceived notions of which exercise you "should" practice or which exercise you may have tried earlier in your life.

Twelve

......

Type 3: Mantra

Mantra is the repetition of a sacred word or words. The root word *man* (*manana*) means "thought" and *tra* means "instrument." The word or sound used for a mantra reverses the usual reason of conveying meaning, whereby the mantra creates a thought. Normally, speech is conveying a thought from one person to another. Mantra uses sound to create a thought; the mantra is a vibration that has its own power. This point cannot be stressed strongly enough because rarely do we realize that sounds can actually create thought. The actual process of mantra meditation, like most ancient meditation techniques, is quite simple. Practicing mantra can be summarized as word repetition.

The repetition of prayers, practiced by most world religions, is the traditional source of affirmations covered in the visualization chapter. A large percentage of people who pray and meditate find reducing the prayer to one sacred word helpful. Thus, it is recommended to gain a familiarity with this practice of repeating one sacred word to enrich one's meditation practice. Since the mantra is vocalized over and over again, it can be used in everyday situations to create a desired thought pattern.

A personal affirmation for healing can also be repeated. The entire exercise consists of repeating a word or short phrase throughout the period of meditation. After some time one actually feels the power of the word in an energetic way. Easwaran discusses the mantra as a phone call to God and teaches that the mantra can penetrate every cell. Let me direct you to Easwaran's book *The Mantram Handbook*, a fantastic resource for this type of meditation, found in the reference section.

This chapter is shorter then the previous two in spite of its potential magnitude. Following your intuition may increase the meaning aspect of the mantra. Do remember that the important element of this course is its emphasis on practicing simple exercises to experience meditation more than intellectual descriptions of meditation. Via firsthand experience, you learn the most effective form of meditation and that meditation is about higher states of consciousness established by simple exercises that focus the mind. Elaborate exercises require much energy and great meditation sages consistently offer simple practices.

Many mantra meditation traditions have elaborate rituals for receiving a personal mantra that are cloaked in secrecy, mystery, and reverence. The private nature of the mantra increases its level of importance and establishes a sacred association with the chosen word. This set of rituals reinforces the power of the word, and when in this process, the system works. Many of these traditions consequently do not recommend choosing one's own mantra. However, high ritual or not, mantra meditation works when the practitioner believes deeply in the chosen word.

Unique Instructions for Mantra Meditation

For mantra meditation, the same teachings from the Eastern Orthodox Church that also use mantra are very effective. Try the following sequence: say the word aloud, whisper the word, move the lips with no sound, repeat the word in the mind, repeat the word in the heart, then feel the word in the entire body until you reach a feeling of oneness with the divine. This word may be repeated during the day. Words like love, peace, joy, hope, a name of God, or other sacred sounds are typical examples of mantras. Thinking about God or the divine instead of thinking other fleeting thoughts fills the mind with inspiration. Repeat the mantra for fifteen to thirty minutes. If the mind wanders, return to the repetition.

Sit quietly, and repeat this word or phrase in your mind over and over for a total of twenty minutes. Notice how you feel during the first few minutes. Then, notice your state of mind around the ten-minute halfway point. Finally, after twenty minutes, observe how this experience affects you. Choose one of the below exercises as the subject for creating your personal mantra.

Exercise 1: Mantra from a Peak Experience

Meditate on your childhood experiences of the sacred, of God or of a powerful moment that transformed you. Find something stellar and summarize that experience into your own mantra. An example might be an experience you had when coming of age around puberty. Many religions offer rites of passage at this time (around the age of thirteen). You may have an early childhood experience of an angel saving your life or of a very old person's love that touched your heart. Think on this experience and call forth the power of this experience by creating a mantra about it. For example, as a child, if you felt the power of love during a difficult time, your mantra could be "the power of love." If you are religious, repeating just the word "faith" could be the entire mantra.

While this course remains secular in its approach, please note that religious mantras are powerful to believers. If you feel a close connection to a particular religious word or deity, by all means, use that ancient mantra or prayer. Equally, nonreligious personal beliefs about the universe may carry power. Common examples are "compassion" with the exhalation, "love" with the inhalation.

If you have any negative associations with spirituality in your past, these issues can be explored by writing in a journal. Try to understand the associated emotions with these experiences. See if you can be objective in the present and understand how the circumstances occurred. If you are able to gain a new perspective on the situation, you may be healed and the stored emotional memory may release or subside. As you go further into meditation, such subtle feelings may arise. Take the time to understand yourself without creating any new unsettling reactions. The forgiveness that you find may be the source of a powerful mantra to enhance the new positive feelings.

Each of the above processes for selecting a personal mantra couples deep-seated beliefs with an energetic vibration. The mantra requires belief to bring meaning to a vibration. Likewise, the belief needs an expression to make itself manifest. The repetition of a sacred sound in a flippant fashion will not serve like a meditation spell. **Belief + Vibration = Mantra Meditation.**

EXERCISE 2: FOCUS ON THE POSITIVE OPPOSITE

A second method of choosing a personal mantra is one from yoga (*Yoga Sutras* II:34) that transforms a personal weakness into inner strength. This exercise begins by focusing on the essence of any stressful situation. Inquire within yourself why the situation causes you stress. If the traffic annoys you, take responsibility for the annoyed reaction and ask why you are annoyed. Most often, the personal response relates to being annoyed by larger issues like having to pay a mortgage and thus working this job that puts you in traffic. Then, you are annoyed that you feel like a failure and ultimately that you have not reached your fullest potential. From this, you fear that your life is passing by so quickly and after some honest reflection, you discover that fear is driving your annoyance.

Once you have figured out a deep-seated reason for the stress (notice that I did not say *the* deep-seated reasons, for there may be multiple!), the *Yoga Sutras* recommend focusing on the "corresponding opposite positive attribute." In this example, self-acceptance may be the one potential opposite. The person would figure out their personal response and then use that positive concept as the material for the mantra. This personal mantra would be a healing force for day-to-day stress as well as a great motive for meditation. Finally, see how this adult choice of mantra parallels the discovery of a childhood spiritual experience as mentioned above.

EXERCISE 3: FROM THE SAGES

Many mantras are derived from sounds that have been heard by sages over the ages. "OM" (or "AUM"), the primordial sound of the universe, is the most pertinent example. In states of profound meditation or *Samadhi* where the ego dissolves for a short time, the meditator may hear this "OM" sound. The meditator loses individuated consciousness during this period of time, even a few heartbeats. Like stories of near-death experiences, some meditators describe hearing the "OM" sound as they gradually return to normal waking consciousness. The repetition of the "OM" sound then calls forth first a connection to the larger universe as well as mimics this profound state of meditation.

Mantra from Scripture, Prayers, or Poetry

Most of the great spiritual traditions share some form of daily scripture study, yet Western culture has lost this tradition in the modern era. However, most cultures of the world rely on scriptures for inspiration, wisdom, and the cultivation of spiritual attitudes. There are many reasons to make scripture reading a priority!

The things we read and think about are like mental sustenance. By listening to the news or reading the newspaper for twenty minutes per day, the mind is filled with sensational headlines or negative thinking. Reading scripture allows the mind to ponder inspiring ideas. When a trying situation comes to mind, we are more likely to remember a scriptural idea. Our erroneous thoughts will be of a more uplifting nature.

If we can discuss scripture with a group of faithful people, our relationships will be based on deeper values. By penetrating the meaning of scriptures deeply, the truth may be applied to our lives. As a person ages, wisdom develops and young people will turn to the wise person for advice. Read the words of the great mystics and sages to help you experience the state of mind of the author—try to live in the saint's robe.

Exercise 4: Passage Meditation
Pick a short passage for meditation. Read and reread the passage until it is familiar or memorized. Continue reading it for five to fifteen minutes. When memorized, you may repeat the scripture reading in your mind with your eyes closed. If one particular word grabs your attention, remain focused on the idea. Notice how you relate to the scripture. How would it be if you were present when the sage uttered the holy words? How do the words convey meaning to your life in the present? Let other creative approaches help you derive meaning from the text. Close your eyes and remain with the state of mind induced by the scripture. If the mind wanders, return to the passage.

Blocks to Mantra Meditation

Imagine saying the same word ten thousand times? How about repeating the same mantra for thirty minutes every day for a year? Just as focusing on the breath is nearly impossible to do without a spiritual backdrop (recall from chapter 10), repeating a word does not entertain the mind with colorful images nor interesting thoughts, thus the mind may feel bored. This boredom is likely a case of attachment to things outside of one's self for happiness. The mind will play all kinds of tricks on you to avoid meditating as the new quiet patterns bump against the busy mind that is being healed. At times the mind may rebel like an annoyed child. The mind may behave in a depressive manner appearing to be in the prison of meditation.

As explained in different areas of this book, meditation is simple but the undisciplined mind is savvy. The number of thought distractions is countless. The mind is very clever with these disturbances, so the advice is to remember that any thought outside of the mantra is a distraction during the meditation session. Do expect to have varieties of these distractions for years; I often say that the experienced meditators are adept at accepting distractions but not reacting to the same. However, if you know that meditation may be difficult at times, you can plan ahead for it. Meditation in a group supports you when you are feeling oppressed just as you inspire others when you are in an inspired state of mind, so it is recommended to try to join a group.

Loss of meaning occurs when a mechanical, rote behavior lacks essence. If you have used a mantra for a period of time, you may lose the deep sense of its original meaning. Using "love" as an example, instead of meditating on the subtle qualities of love, the mind may remain at a superficial level—which is actually meditation on the sound of the word and not the meaning. Mantra includes a sacred sound *and* a sacred intention.

Daydreaming may occur in any form of meditation. In the case of mantra, you may think of two thoughts at the same time, especially when one act is repetition. The prayer, "Be still and know that I am God," may be reduced to "Be still." A simple mantra may continue on while in your mind you plan what to eat for lunch. Let the mantra echo in the background of your thoughts. This daily emphasis of the mantra aids the discipline of meditation to focus on one thought.

Mantra Meditation for Daily Life

A young thirteenth-century Christian monk, Brother Lawrence, wrote the classic *The Practice of the Presence of God* (Spire, 1958). In his new monastery, Brother Lawrence requested any job other than kitchen work. As a means for personal growth, the elder monks sent Lawrence to the kitchen. For years, he detested the clanging pots and pans, but the young monk ardently coped with kitchen work. In time, Brother Lawrence writes that he was able to witness the presence of God even in the kitchen amidst the noise of pots and pans. After years of perseverance, he was able to find the same piety in the kitchen as in the chapel. Such an example may inspire us to find peace in situations that appear lifeless to us, for our experience of the divine is internal.

Brother Lawrence faced his hardships directly. After his calling to lead a religious life at a monastery, he was stuck in the kitchen. This thrust Lawrence into a period of gloom, a gloom that he had no choice but to face daily amidst banging of pots and pans. After much soul-searching, Lawrence chose to alter his view of reality and perceive peace in a noisy place.

The image known as "the dark night of the soul" is taught by St. John of the Cross, a seventeenth century Spanish mystic. The experience of darkness or emptiness provides an environment in which the mind can not grasp at distractions. Brother Lawrence's long suffering in the kitchen forced him into the "dark night" predicament where his mind could find no comfortable distraction. Most people's lives have difficult areas that act as a dark night. Viewed from a superficial perspective, our difficulties can be the root of undue suffering, or we can use our difficulties for spiritual growth. Eventually, as these mystics demonstrate, one's difficulties may be utilized as a means for spiritual growth by teaching us to focus less on our mind and more on the super-consciousness of reality. As St. John of the Cross writes: "I entered not knowing where, I remained not knowing/Beyond all science knowing … It was peace, it was love, it was perfect knowledge/ In deep loneliness, I saw with wisdom …"

In *Testament of Devotion* (36) Thomas Kelly writes:

Walk and talk and work and laugh with your friends. But behind
the scenes, keep up the life of simple prayer and inward worship.
Keep it up throughout the day. Let inward prayer be your last act
before you fall asleep and the first act when you awake…Lapses
and forgettings are so frequent. Our surroundings grow so exciting.
Our occupations are so exacting. But when you catch yourself again,
lose no time in self-recriminations, but breathe a silent prayer for
forgiveness and begin again, just where you are.

Apply your mantra to working situations to create a positive thought. This asserts that you have the power to influence your experience of all situations, even situations where stress appears to prevail.

EXERCISE 5: MANTRA FOR WORK
The foundation exercises of this course apply clear thinking to mundane stresses such as waiting in line, driving, and washing the dishes. Beyond making these mundane, boring, tiresome chores pleasing, attempt to cultivate a selfless feeling while doing these tasks. Hum a spiritual song or recite your mantra during the task.

During your meditation, begin the process with three minutes of reflection of a chore or situation that you plan to improve. Notice how memories of this chore create a conflict inside of you. Begin with a mantra that reverses this trend and makes you feel at peace in the same situation. Remain reminded of a reality larger than the mind or ego. One ninety-year-old woman used to say that when she baked, cleaned, and cared for others, she was communing with all the people over the ages that baked, cleaned, and cared for others. Her mantra was "Oneness with all." Open your mind to inspiring insights as you perform your daily chores. To explore this mindset, pick one stressful situation tomorrow and an exact time to recite your mantra for a few minutes. Obviously, the task must be mundane like driving or washing the dishes or preparing for a meeting.

Summary

Each type-specific chapter in this book is merely a summary of a much more involved meditation path. After practicing as suggested in this chapter, take a pause for reflection and answer the following questions.

1. What stood out as significant for you in this chapter's practices?

2. Do you have any insight about why these were important for you? Do they relate to habitual patterns?

3. Note any other reasons why that certain exercise resonated with you.

4. Did this exercise help you becoming more aware of the interplay of thoughts and emotions?

5. What exercise felt right?

Use your intuition or gut reaction to this. Try to remove preconceived notions of which exercise you "should" practice or which exercise you may have tried earlier in your life.

Thirteen

Type 4: Devotion, Prayer, or Intentionality

Originally when I learned meditation in Japan, prayer was not taught. While considered a mind-quieting activity, prayer was never given as equal with meditation in terms of reaching higher states of consciousness like nirvana. During my time in India, I had many spiritually based experiences that were cloaked in religious images from my childhood. Although raised as a Roman Catholic, I had not been to a church in three years, yet still I was drawn to familiar prayers. I was understanding biblical truths while immersed in the study yoga in India; it was a cross-cultural experience to say the least! As my studying and teaching continued, I found myself drawn to continue the journey with a concentration in spirituality with the Quakers at the Earlham School of Religion's seminary.

As a graduate student, one of my teaching assistant jobs was leading pass/fail yoga courses. The number of students began at fifteen and grew to sixty per semester. Upon hearing of the yoga classes' popularity, the open-minded campus minister told me that the students enrolled in yoga were never seen at any Sunday church services. We realized that through the meditative yoga classes, the students were not only learning about the health benefits of yoga, but they were connecting to something larger than themselves. When I would lead the meditation portion of the class, many student responses were based on their childhood experiences of prayer. This led me to understand that a large group of people who are not outwardly religious may be inwardly using prayer as their method of meditation.

Therefore, further research into prayer reveals that a large number of people automatically quiet their mind in a relational manner. They may not pray to the deity of their upbringing in all cases, but they are still reaching out in a personal way to the object of their meditation. This is very different from the type of meditation that is defined as focus on one thought. Prayer concerns a relationship between two parties: your higher power and you. Independent of whether or not you consider yourself religious, it is possible you have a mind wired for prayer.

Prayer Is More Listening, Less Talking

The level of prayer discussed herein has more to do with listening than talking. The focus of the prayer is relational; however, the person praying is in a receptive mindset, waiting until the higher power, deity, nature, or whatever else it is called resonates. This is very key as you may deepen a feeling of appreciation of nature by stating, "Thank you for this beautiful creation" and then dwell on that thought awaiting a response, be it a feeling from nature, a shift in consciousness, or a closeness to the divine. You may make a prayer of healing and hold the mind on the prayer for a long period of time. You may ask for help from God and then wait with appreciative patience. Before journeying with prayer and intentionality, the psychological dimension is important to understand and heal if necessary.

Relationship to the Concept
of a Higher Power (or God)

In this section on prayer/intentionality as a mode of meditation, the topic of God is discussed freely. Over the years, I have met people who were blocked from their natural meditative practice due to negative experiences with organized religion. Likewise, I have met people who have made great strides in other forms of meditation by understanding their view of the divine. Especially if you feel any resistance to God or religion, please complete the exercises in this chapter. These exercises have helped hundreds of people develop improved clarity and self-understanding.

Firstly, note that you are urged to name or discover your personal religious beliefs as a facet of your meditation. No beliefs are forced nor promoted beyond the point that self-understanding improves meditative absorption. Your spiritual beliefs (be they with God, a higher power, another religious affiliation, or atheistic/agnostic) are held deeply in your psyche. From this depth, you can derive tremendous energy for meditative focus. When you **believe** deeply in something, concentration around that belief can be powerful. The goal is to channel that deep level of concentration in meditation practice. To facilitate this, please answer the following questions in your journal.

1. Who was God to you during your childhood years?

2. Who is God to you presently and how do you feel about God?

3. What is the meaning of life?

4. What happens when a person dies?

5. Do you have a soul or spirit?

6. Do you belong to any religious or spiritual grounded groups presently and what beliefs link you to that group?

(Note that anonymous groups, nature clubs, religious organizations, yoga or martial arts groups, and the like are all spiritually based.)

Secondly, note that personal resistance to aspects of religious belief may be revealed during your meditation practice. Because powerful emotions are evoked by personal religious beliefs, conflicts with religious beliefs or unresolved spiritual experiences can stifle meditation experiences. As the mind becomes very quiet, deep-seated beliefs and feelings rise to conscious understanding. Healing or resolution of previous sentiments can help free a person in blocks to meditation. These practices help to overcome any limiting beliefs and accept the religions as they are. Below are questions that may help in the healing or resolution of religious issues:

1. What was your childhood experience of religion and God?

2. How do you cope with conflicting messages from the religions that claim superiority over other religions? How about the religions that condone violence or other unethical behaviors?

3. Have you ever been personally misled or emotionally hurt by a religious group? Most importantly, can you forgive or release that experience?

4. Are you at peace with the religious tradition of your childhood? (Please be aware of and compassionate to the fact that these above questions, if not an issue for you, are an issue for a high portion of the meditation population and are important to uncover for effective meditation.)

5. Can you forgive any issues that may linger from your childhood spiritual experiences?

If any of these are challenging questions, please consult a professional who may guide you in the process of reclaiming your spiritual heritage.

Devotion to a Higher Power or God

As mentioned above, our beliefs about life hold tremendous power in the psyche. These beliefs are planted in our consciousness from an early stage of life by our parents, our religious institutions and our culture. When you are part of a belief system, it is helpful to recognize it as such, and be aware that it is only one framework for accessing higher consciousness. This type of intentionality and prayer is not the superficial supplication wishing for good times and material blessings. The prayer that relates to meditative absorption includes a rapport between the divine and the person praying. From that relationship, the prayer may speak to the divine and then remain silent for long durations.

The *Yoga Sutras* offer instructions on this type of meditation:

To feel always that I am doing everything as if being prompted by Him is what is known as surrendering everything to God. The saying, 'Whatever I do, willingly or unwillingly, I am offering its fruits, whether happiness or misery, to you' means that 'I do not want either happiness or sorrow nor shall be perturbed by either. Everything is being done by you.' This frame of mind banishes all egotistic feelings and brings about a perpetual faith in God.
—Aranya, 1981, 56

From a nontheistic perspective, this can be thought of as relinquishing our ego with the intention to enter into communion with the world. Li Po, one of the greatest Chinese poets of premodern times, offers an exquisite example:

The birds have vanished into the sky and now the last cloud drains away. We sit together, the mountain and me, Until only the mountain remains.

If praying to God or meditating on a statue or landscape gives you inner peace, keep doing it. The forms of devotion are vast. When you are able to find a relationship to the divine that is fulfilling, use these strong beliefs to dedicate all of your energy to God or a higher power. It is recommended that you maintain a connection to one's religious heritage, as your past influences are present. As mentioned in the exercise from chapter 11 on visualization, it is helpful to have peace with the religion of your childhood even if you do not practice that particular path presently.

Many Western people who are attracted to meditation find the divine in nature, and if shamanistic practices had been available, those types of natural worship would have been very fulfilling. Devoting your mind to nature is another way of going beyond the ego-sense into a larger reality. By observing nature around you, focus on connection: notice how the breath you exhale is inhaled by the tree, the water you drink comes from the earth and the clouds. We each have specialized roles in modern society, unlike the people of one hundred years ago. In the past, we chopped wood, grew food, and interacted with wildlife. The computer-age person can sit in front of a machine and use money to buy everything he or she needs. Thus, you may live in a human sphere and never go beyond your boundaries. By relating to nature, make this a dedicated study. Camping trips or outdoor hikes can be treated as spiritual experiences. A devotional feeling toward the divine essence of the natural world can expand one's consciousness. For example, yoga postures performed with a devout attitude may serve as a form of body prayer, and some poses may be held for a longer duration in this mindset.

Here are a few possibilities (from many) for you to experiment with devotional practices.

EXERCISE 1: GAZING AT A SPIRITUAL OBJECT
Choose an object for devotion or meditation. Gazing passively at a revered picture or a nature scene are both good for reaching a peaceful

state. You may begin by gazing at the flame of a candle or a statue. Slowly close your eyes and feel in your heart that your entire being is united with the object of your meditation. Our mind separates us from things by distinguishing our being as different from things outside of us. In profound devotion, the subject and object merge into one. If your mind wanders, however, you may open the eyes to come back to the meditation. Thereafter, close the eyes to focus within again.

EXERCISE 2: REFLECT ON YOUR PERSONAL SPIRITUAL BELIEFS

Deep reflection in a prayerlike manner can be a method of following your heart into a profound meditative consciousness. The temptation to daydream exists in this method if you continue to think for the entire session. If you feel prone to constant thinking, take up a journal to list your thoughts and meditate when you begin to feel more quietude in your mind and life. Otherwise, consider your deeper beliefs and relation to the divine for the first five minutes and then commune with this in your heart for a silent prayer.

EXERCISE 3: PRAYING TO GOD OR A HIGHER POWER

Sit quietly and discuss a topic with your higher power. Allow room there for longer periods of silence. Focus your mind on the mind of God, and discover how you pray. You may feel free to pray for others or in any fashion from your personal spiritual practices.

EXERCISE 4: BODY PRAYER RELAXATION IN CHILD'S POSE OR PROSTRATION POSE

Explore relaxation in Child's Pose or in a prostration posture. Both poses begin kneeling with the torso draped over the folded legs, forehead coming to or approaching the floor. If you have any knee troubles, you may simply lie on the stomach. For the Child's Pose, place your arms alongside the torso. This posture and the curve of the spine it induces mimics the child within the womb, evoking a feeling of safety and protection. For the prostration posture, place your arms above the shoulders. This creates a stronger feeling of surrender. Breathe into the diaphragm area allowing for tranquility of mind and a gentle lower-back opening for the body.

Prayer in Nature, Connection to Nature

Communion with the elements of nature is another method of prayer. Many meditation practitioners feel close to the natural world, be they religious or not. The natural world offers a peaceful tranquility and order as all elements of the landscape relate to one another in a sym-biotic fashion. Using this feeling of being a part of nature harmonizes the human being's ego with the larger world. In some practitioners, this relationship to the natural world leads to a very quiet mind. Experiment with these types of practices to see how it fits for you.

The purpose of this lesson is to introduce prayer in the context of communing with nature. There are a variety of shamanic practices (too numerous to cover here), but hopefully this type of introduction can encourage those who feel this interest. To expand your knowledge of the shamanic practices, refer to the book *Meditation: The Complete Guide* by Monaghan and Diereck.

In the United States is a centuries-old history (as with most world cultures) of the relationship with nature. Native American cultures, the source of many shamanic practices, lived in harmony with their natural surroundings. Their spirituality hinged on a relationship to nature.

Modern settlers in America were inspired by the work and study of Ralph Waldo Emerson's approach to contemplation that empha-sizes connecting to nature. Emerson, along with Henry David Thoreau, founded the Transcendental Club where the first documented study of the yogic text the Bhagavad Gita was noted in the United States. Asian philosophical ideas have influenced the West in the philosophy of Emerson and Thoreau's writings and in psychology through Carl

Jung's works (Coward, 1985). (Note: Swami Vivekananda was the first yogi to present in the USA.)

In "The American Scholar," Emerson defines three stages for the Transcendentalist's life.

1. One studies the wisdom of the past.

   In terms of meditation, a review of major mystics satisfies study of the past.

2. One spiritualizes life by communing with nature and learning to listen to the divine from within one's self.

   This idea closely resembles the yogic thought of stilling one's mind in order to gain an understanding of higher aspects of one's self and reality. Mystics assert that divinity can be found from within.

3. After self-renewal, one works toward the renewal of society at large.

This brief summary of the Transcendentalist teachings may inspire those interested to study further if you find meditative moments in nature inspiring. This type of meditation is considered a type of prayer where there is an active dialogue between the subject (you) and the object (nature)—see the exercises below. The ultimate discovery in this type of prayer lies in the higher state of contemplation where the boundaries between the subject and the object begin to dissolve or merge into oneness. The end of this journey reflects that of the goal of meditation. Note that prayer offers an active dialogue between the subject and object *prior* to the higher states of silence.

Before attempting the following exercise, take a few moments to write any special highlights of your relationship to nature. Do you feel moved by any animals? Consider taking a silent walk outdoors to see the divine in nature. Align your breathing and feel part of that divinity.

EXERCISE 5: MEDITATION ON AN ASPECT OF NATURE

Follow step two of the Transcendentalist path as explained above. If possible, meditate outside or near the window where you may feel close to nature. Clear your mind by breathing in fresh air; as you breathe feel one with the air. Notice that the air and your body are connected as the elements of the air enters your bloodstream. Focus your mind on one aspect of nature and allow the duality between you and the nature object to dissolve. The wind, moon, sun, trees, flowers, insects, rocks, animals, or your breathing can be the object of your meditation. In calm weather, try to practice meditation outdoors. In cold weather, try viewing a fire. Use the senses at first to notice your connection, then progressively let go of the external senses (close the eyes) and find an internal communion with the object you choose.

Contemplative Prayer, Mysticism, and Meditation

Mysticism refers to consciousness of the transcendent, ultimate reality or God consciousness. Mysticism is the highest level of prayer when the prayer and the object prayed to merge in oneness. Like meditation, mysticism crosses religious boundaries, transcending human rules and regulations by direct communion with the divine.

In his classic *The Varieties of Religious Experience*, William James defines mysticism in four facets: ineffability, noetic quality, transiency, and passivity. The ineffable quality of mysticism refers to the inability to explain what occurs in the mystical states of consciousness. This is due to a heightened awareness of reality that is beyond the intellect. Thus, we have mystical poetry and paradoxical sayings from the saints and sages. As Lao Tzu wrote in the *Tao Te Ching*, "Tao can be talked about, but not the Eternal Tao. Names can be named, but not the Eternal Name" (Wu, 1989).

Noetic or "higher knowing" occurs in mystical experience as a deep understanding of the truth of spiritual matters as they begin to unfold. Similarly, in yoga one may attain complete knowledge of a subject or an object by focusing on that topic and entering into a mystical state of consciousness where one transcends the intellect.

James asserts that the third and fourth qualities are less sharply marked. Transiency means that mystical states last for a maximum of thirty minutes and cannot be sustained longer except in rare instances. Passivity describes the state in which a higher power or God over-whelms the mystic. The mystical experiences humble the mystic due to the awe that is experienced by a state of consciousness that the mind cannot fathom.

James also discusses how the mystic is "invulnerable." The mystic may be placed in jail or in the mountains yet no one may control their spirit. James notes that although the mystics may have strong opin-ions, they are still human beings, and the opinions of nonmystics are equally valuable.

In *Practical Mysticism*, Evelyn Underhill outlines a simple three-step mystical process described as immanence, transcendence, and pure con-templation. Note the common element to Emerson's three steps above.

First, one attempts to see God in all things in the world by perceiv-ing the divine essence of all beings and things. In other words, when you can see the divinity of an evildoer, you can see God in all things. Secondly, as one develops the ability to know the transcendent view of the divine without tangible explanation, one has a sense of a higher reality. Lastly, one quits striving; the mind is steadfast in a divine pres-ence and all the mystic does is "be" in a contemplative state of mind. Grace alone transports the mystic in this last stage of contemplation.

Exercise 6: Practicing Contemplation
In following the three-step process for contemplative prayer:

1. Focus on your understanding of the divine from an immanent way. Pray a prayer of thanksgiving for the divine aspects of life. Try to feel your connection to the divine by praying from your heart.

2. Once you feel this connection in the heart, begin to expand the connection to a universal perspective. Focus on the mind in stage two. Do not dismiss the heartfelt feelings, but expand the feelings to connect all living beings. See the global or universal nature of the divine. Your prayer has ceased to be individual and now includes the world. This step requires many levels of acceptance and understanding that your personal view of life is limited by your own unique experiences. This step allows you to grow beyond your own personal beliefs.

3. Once you feel at peace with both your own heart and the universe, then it is time to cease striving. Just be. Please be aware that you may not reach this step immediately. If you attempt to cease striving but end up with a rash of thoughts, then return to step one. If you feel very quiet in this state, remain there for up to twenty minutes.

EXERCISE 7: JOURNALING MYSTICAL EXPERIENCE

In light of the three stages of mysticism (the immanent, the transcendent, and the contemplative) reflect on your own place in the continuum. You may devise your own steps for mysticism.

- How do you relate to the divine?

- Do you find solace in the immanence of natural settings?

- Do you see the divine operating in your daily life?

- Do you have a sense of a transcendent reality?

- Can you see the larger picture in life and step back from the activities in your life to perceive reality purely?

- Are you learning how to accept reality in such a way that your meditation is passive?

Healing with Prayer: Healing Light

The healing prayer aspects of many spiritual traditions use the image of light to represent life force or bioenergy. The process resembles visualization affirmations, except the image is another person or a cause. The subject-object relationship exists in prayer, whereas visualization is based on imagination. Depending on the individual meditator's disposition, the light image surrounding the person receiving the blessing may take different forms, however this type of prayer is not limited to images as feelings and thoughts are appropriate expressions. Common examples are light surrounding the other, keeping the thought of the other in your heart, and a beam of energy from a source of healing to the other.

While the skeptic inside of your rational mind may not believe in healing prayer, a series of scientific studies have proven prayer effective. In San Francisco, cardiologist Randolph Byrd used the standard double-blind procedures to study 393 heart patients prayed for by nuns in a certain convent. The results were astounding: the prayed-for group was five times less likely to require antibiotics and three times less likely to develop pulmonary edema (Byrd, 1988). If research is not enough for the rational mind, the fact that people have been praying for thousands of years in most spiritual traditions reflects a large community supporting the practice.

For this and most other types of prayer, intention is the first step. The person focusing on the light has to clear the mind initially. Preparation revolves around first praying for your personal health. Exercises from part II of this book serve as good mind-body clearing exercises.

Simple stretching is good for the body. Relaxation focuses on a healing light for your body and mind.

The biggest block for prayer surrounds the personal desire for the illness or imbalance to go away immediately. However, an idea of when a person *should* (note the emphasis) be healthy does not account for all possibilities—perhaps an added week of rest may help the person emotionally. Paradoxically, a specific wish in this situation does not align with universal laws. "Unspecified prayers for a long duration" according to the Spindrift Studies prove the most effective results (Owen, 1988, 22-23). Thus, a thought like "I surround my friend with universal energy" works, but the wish "I send light to heal my friend's leg" is limited. The universe has a knowing higher than the individual conscious mind. Simply offer an unspecified prayer.

Once the broad intention is achieved, imagine your heart and mind as a channel of light. Hold the image of your friend or cause in your mind for one, five, or twenty minutes. Attempt to remain a passive channel focused on positive energy without attachment to results. Like our visualization exercises, you may have a unique version of the light. Some see white light around the person. Others see colors, and still others feel energy without strong visual images.

A third process relates to listening deeply to your higher self or intuitive thinking. Respect intuitive thoughts and when appropriate, act on these ideas.

Overcoming Worry

If you worry about a difficult situation, use this worry as a signal to visualize a healing light to bless the situation. The worry signals a dire situation that concerns you. If the worry persists, it creates distress in the worrier and fear related to the situation. If the worry reminds you to offer another prayer, then the worry has been channeled in a positive direction.

Healing Prayer Summary

1. Clear your mind.

2. Reflect on the prayer; be reasonable and open-minded.

3. Remain focused on the prayer for the duration. Long duration intensifies the prayer.

4. The goal is communion with your higher power as you see it.

5. Do not minimize the prayer by wishing for an outcome.

6. Origin of sickness can be on any level: physical, mental, emotional, or spiritual.

7. Healing is more than physical.

8. Wellness is not the goal; communion with the higher power/ God is the goal.

Reasons Why Prayer Does Not Work

- A lack of faith.

- Suffering communicates the need for transformation.

- Belief blocks healing.

- Denial of the underlying issue.

- Praying for wrong issue.

- Praying for symptoms to go away, instead of the root.

- Incorrect time.

- You are not the healer in the dynamic.

- Social situation blocks healing.

- Person feels unworthy of healing.

Exercise 8: Healing Light

1. Apply the healing light to your mind and body by stretching, breathing lightly in and out and letting relaxation surround your body with light.

2. Apply the healing light prayer to a person or situation in need.

3. Focus on a difficult personal situation or on anyone you feel anger toward. Attempt to understand the situation fully to release the pain and cultivate forgiveness. Allow this to soften the situation and allow healing in your self. For some examples, you may forgive those who created a war internally, but you do not have to join that war. You may forgive a criminal, but you don't have to give the thief the key to the bank safe.

Summary

Each type-specific chapter in this book is merely a summary of a much more involved meditation path. After practicing as suggested in this chapter, take a pause for reflection and answer the following questions.

1. What stood out as significant for you in this chapter's practices?

2. Do you have any insight about why these were important for you? Do they relate to habitual patterns?

3. Note any other reasons why that certain exercise resonated with you.

4. Did this exercise help you become more aware of the interplay of thoughts and emotions?

5. What exercise felt right?

Use your intuition or gut reaction to this. Try to remove preconceived notions of which exercise you "should" practice or which exercise you may have tried earlier in your life.

Fourteen

Type 5: Mindfulness Meditation

In this course, five types of concentration meditation techniques are discussed, namely: breathing, visualization, mantra, intentionality/prayer (covered in the previous chapters), and contemplative inquiry (the chapter to follow). In concentration meditation exercises, the mind focuses on one thing and ignores other stimuli. The concentrative forms of meditation create a disciplined mind. Once the mind develops maturity in meditation and remains focused with little effort, the object of meditation can itself become a distraction. As practice progresses, various meditative states arise, and the yoga tradition discusses varying levels of meditative absorption (*samadhi*).

The practice of mindfulness is a bit different, though. It uses two modes, concentration and awareness. Initially, we begin by observing the breath, noticing its qualities such as duration, depth, and roughness or smoothness. Then we concentrate on the breath in one particular area, either at the nostrils, in the heart center or in the lower abdomen. After concentration is firmly established, we shift into awareness mode, becoming aware of sensations such as sounds, emotions, and thoughts. Finally, we focus on the impermanent nature of all things.

Mindfulness practice is derived from the Buddhist practice of *Vipassana*, or insight meditation. This type of meditation originated in Southeast Asia, and Buddhist monk Thich Nhat Hanh has inspired many to adopt this practice, which serves as a foundational practice for many Buddhists.

Siddharta Gotama, known as the Buddha (which means "Awakened One"), was born in India to a priestly, wealthy Brahmin family. The Buddha practiced various forms of yoga including asceticism (harsh religious disciplines, such as fasting, seclusion, and arduous spiritual exercise). He simplified the practices of yoga into a meditation on the breath, bypassing discursive modes of thinking so that the nature of reality can be experientially realized. Buddha's methods were a reaction to the excessive and sometimes superstitious forms of ritual that were practiced by many religious sects. Instead of posing the question "What do you believe?" he was more concerned with asking practitioners to notice: "What did you do?" and "How did you do it?" His practice was geared to assist practitioners to realize a state of Nirvana, or unbinding from the fetters of grasping, aversion, and delusion.

Foundational to Buddhist practice is the understanding of interdependence. In *The Heart of Understanding*, Thich Nhat Hanh explains the term "interbeing" which helps remove the interpreting mind from experience:

> *If you are a poet, you will see clearly that there is a cloud floating in this sheet of paper. Without a cloud, there will be no rain; without rain, the trees cannot grow, and without trees, we cannot make paper. The cloud is essential for the paper to exist. If the cloud is not here, the sheet of paper cannot be here either. So we can say that the cloud and the paper "inter-are."*
>
> —Hanh, 1988, 3

This concept is known as interdependent origination—nothing exists in and of itself; everything is dependent upon everything else in the cosmos.

The Western-trained mind normally prides itself in distinguishing one thing from another. Philosophical discussions honor subtle distinctions in order to better differentiate things. Science has capitalized on the mind's ability to reverse the ancient ways of seeing nature interwoven in all things, by distinguishing matter into groups of atoms. One task for meditation practitioners is to function in a world of distinctions while simultaneously residing in the awareness of the interconnectedness of all things.

In mindfulness practice, we learn to observe physical sensations and mental processes, thus expanding our awareness of interconnectivity. The purpose is to attend fully to the present moment without our habitual filters of concepts, judgment, expectations, or cultural assumptions—without our "story" about what we are experiencing. With practice we begin to gain clarity about our experience without our own chronic interpretations or socially conditioned ways of being. As we develop practice both on the cushion and in daily life, insight into the impermanent nature of reality arises. We are able to see the constructed nature of the ego, and become less bound by beliefs of an abiding "self."

Mindfulness is not aimed at learning anything external, knowledge, or information. Its aim is to help us discover that which is inherently within. Our minds are naturally open and unobstructed, but they become clouded by any or all of the following: attachment to desires (greed), aversion or hostility, or the deluded misperception of reality. Our minds are also clouded by the ego's tendency to manipulate things for our own advantage. As we practice, our relationship with the ego personality shifts; we discover that everything is impermanent. With everything in a state of flux, there is really no fixed identity, no sense of "self" to cling to.

EXERCISE 1: FOCUS ON THE BREATH

Sit comfortably in a meditation posture either on the floor or in a chair. Set a timer for fifteen minutes, so that you need not have to concern yourself with time. Begin to adjust your gaze: your eyes may be open, gazing downward at a 45-degree angle, or closed completely. Begin to note the qualities of the breath. Are the inhalations and exhalations long or short? Is the breath rough and choppy, or smooth? Are you breathing deeply, or is the breathing shallow? Does it feel moist or dry? After noting the qualities, focus your attention on the breath in one particular area, either at the nostrils, the center of the chest or in the lower abdomen. Keep the attention focused there, and count the breaths at the end of each exhalation. You may count up to ten, and then back down to zero. Repeat this process, keeping focused and steady. If the mind wanders, return it gently but firmly to the breath.

Awareness of Sensation: Connecting with the Body

As we experience life, we generally tend to judge experiences as pleasant, unpleasant, or neutral. When a pleasant sensation arises, we want more of it. When something we judge unpleasant arises, we want to avoid it at all costs. And when something neutral arises, we hardly pay any attention to it at all. Much of our life is lived unconsciously of the pulls of greed (attachment to desires) and aversion (which can range from simple avoidance to downright hostility). We are also largely unaware of the vast range of experiences we interpret as neutral, because they simply do not command our immediate attention.

In mindfulness, we train to become aware of sensations and how we navigate our life based on our relationship to them. As practice progresses, we can more readily see how our judgments and perceptions influence each other. We become more attuned to subtleties, and more open to experience. During the day, it is important to become aware of how we are carrying our bodies. We give mindful attention to our posture while sitting or standing, notice and release hunching of the shoulders, tensions in the forehead, or clenching in the jaw, for example. We become aware of physical constriction, and focus on greater fluidity in motion. The following exercises will help us attune to these subtleties:

Exercise 2: The Body Scan for Physical Mindfulness

Remove your shoes and lie on your back on a mat or towel on the floor. Start to move towards a relaxed and comfortable position. You may choose to have your legs extended (a pillow under the knees may feel comfortable) or have your knees bent with your feet near your bottom. Closing your eyes, begin to draw your attention inward. Notice the gentle rising and falling of the belly with each breath, in and out. There is no effort to breathe in a particular way. During this body scan, maintain an attitude of curiosity and investigation. If you notice the mind wandering, or if thoughts should arise, simply return your attention to the body scan.

1. Bringing your awareness to the crown of your head, see if you can notice the presence of any sensations.

2. Shift your awareness downward, noticing the muscles around the eyes, and the area between the eyebrows. Notice the cheeks, the jaw, and the tongue resting in the mouth.

3. See if you can locate the center of the skull, a point midway between the eyes and the back of the head, the crown and the jaw. Are you aware of any sensations here?

4. Drawing your attention downward into the throat, do you notice any constriction, or does the passage of air seem smooth and flowing?

5. Notice the muscles of the neck and the vertebrae.

6. Notice any sensations or feelings in the shoulders. Slowly extend awareness down the arms, pausing to notice the joints of the elbows and wrists. Extend your awareness into the hands, then the fingers.

7. Remember that if you find your mind wandering, simply return your attention to the body scan.

8. Next, bringing your attention to the front of the body, notice any sensations present in the lungs or ribcage. Sometimes sensations can be felt as areas of compression or tightness, and sometimes certain colors present themselves. This is fine, simply continue to observe. You may sense your heartbeat or the rise and fall of the breath.

9. Moving your attention downward to the abdominal area, focus on what sensations may be present there. Do you sense movement? Are there areas of compression or constriction?

10. Bringing attention to the back of the body, notice any sensations present in the spine and shoulder blades, the middle of the back, and the lower back. Resist naming the sensations, simply note and experience them.

11. Move your attention to the sitting bones, your waist and hips. Bring your awareness to the pelvic floor, and the area of the groin and genitals.

12. Allow your focus to extend down your legs, noticing the thighs, hamstrings, and knees.

13. Continue noticing the calves and shins, the ankles and feet.

14. Focus on the balls of the feet, then the arches, and finally the heels.

15. Notice the feeling of your feet on the floor, the steady grounding it provides.

16. Begin noticing your entire body as one interconnected system.

17. Feel the rise and fall of the breath throughout the entire body

18. Allow yourself to inhabit your body fully; relaxed and yet alert to the present moment.

19. Become aware that all these sensations, all these feelings are flowing freely. None of them are permanent.

20. When you are ready, begin to wiggle your fingers and toes. Gently open your eyes. Remain fully connected to the present moment as you arise and go about your day.

EXERCISE 3: MEDITATIVE WALKING FOR FOCUS AND FLUIDITY

Experiment with these ways of walking ands see what happens to the bodily sensations as the focus shifts. First begin walking very, very slowly, concentrating on the soles of the feet. Notice the placement of each foot as it touches the ground. With each footfall, notice the sequence of motion of the parts of the foot. Notice the distribution of weight, the shifts necessary to remain balanced, and how navigation feels at this slow pace. Walk this way for two minutes.

Next begin to pick up the pace to a moderate walking speed. Shift your focus to the heart center and imagine you are being pulled forward gently by a light string attached there. As you practice, a sense of gliding may emerge. Walk this way for two minutes. Now start to shift your focus once again: imagine there is a bowl which is nearly full of water resting in your pelvic area. As you walk, allow the water to slosh gently from side to side without spilling. Focus on the area of the navel and walk at a moderate pace, conscious of bringing greater fluidity into your movements.

Questions for Consideration

- What did you notice about the ways attention was focused?

- What did you notice about fluidity and constriction?

- Did you notice an ability to be present in the body in different ways?

Observing the Interplay of Thoughts and Emotions

Another aspect of mindfulness is to bring greater awareness to feelings and emotions. We can train ourselves to understand different feelings and the ways that they function. When we do, we can understand how to prevent the conditions that lead to painful, disruptive, or confused emotional states, simply by relaxing and altering our relationship to what is happening.

We often think that people or situations outside us are responsible for how we feel. Our language clearly reflects this misperception. You may often hear someone say, "She made me so angry when she…" There is, for most, almost always the attempt to blame another person or situation for our emotional state. How different it would be to take responsibility for our reactivity: "I allowed myself to become upset when she…"

Mindfulness meditation practice provides the mental training to shift from reactivity to response. In a reactive situation, we are "locked in" to the prevailing emotion. It seems to have control over us. With mindfulness, we develop the ability to step back a bit, pause, and witness the emotion. Once we can do so, we can choose a response rather than being locked in to reactivity.

Emotions have two components, sensations and thoughts. These often operate at a level below consciousness. Mindfulness helps us become more aware of their interplay. Pause for a moment and try this little exercise.

Exercise 4: Words and Feelings
Read the following words one at a time, and then pause. Give yourself time to notice what thoughts and sensations arise:

- fire

- spiders

- snow

- pus

- cool water

- apples

- oozing mud

- beauty

If you are observant, you will have noticed how simple words can instigate a variety of sensations and images. In mindfulness, we become more aware of this as a process of impersonal internal events. We develop a curiosity about what is happening and are less likely to be fooled by our habitual patterns of thought, or our usual ways of reacting. We open up to the new possibilities of the moment with freshness and curiosity.

EXERCISE 5: FOCUSING ON LIKES FOR SELF-AWARENESS
For one whole week, take a little time each day to notice one thing that you like. Jot these down in your journal. Again, focus on *noticing* things you like. Also key in and notice the bodily sensations that accompany this experience. The next week, jot down something that happened each day you did not like. What bodily sensations were present then?

Our task is again to find out what we actually feel, and not overlay it with some idea about what we "should" feel. The key here is actually *feeling* the feelings. With practice, we see that emotions are often complex. Sometimes our thoughts are at variance with what we are experiencing. In time we can begin to have some distance from our emotions, and we can choose to respond rather than react. If you are caught in a reactive mode, try this practice, easily remembered with the mnemonic anagram STAR:

Stop
Take a breath
Attend to bodily sensations
Respond rather than react

The response at this point may be simply to do nothing, or it may require mindful speech or mindful action. The capacity to respond mindfully develops each time we experience strong feelings in meditation. We simply allow them to be as they are. As you bring mindful awareness to your life both on the cushion and off, this practice will help you navigate with greater ease and clarity.

The capacity to respond mindfully grows in strength each time we experience strong feelings and emotions during meditation. We work at letting them simply be there just as they are without reacting. Gradually, we begin to learn that effective emotional navigation arises from acceptance and openness to our feelings. In time, we greet life experiences with more calmness because we do not struggle against them, wish things to be other than they are, or have expectations about how things "should" be. We do not have to suppress emotions because they feel too uncomfortable or overwhelming. As we begin to accept ourselves, we find that acceptance of others increases as well, and that compassion for ourselves and others flows more readily and easily.

Working with States of Mind and Beliefs

At any point in our lives and meditation journeys, it becomes a challenge to experience the mind thoroughly, with whatever level of clarity we have. Sometimes we believe our thoughts and think they are an accurate representation of reality. We think that if we think something, then that is the way it is. The bonds of relationship, the dictates of society, and the laws of government all require the ability to see clearly in order to choose how we are going to act in the face of sometimes conflicting demands. This clarity allows for much greater freedom, and sometimes involves great risk. Some of the most difficult choices we make concern "going against the flow" of family expectations, or social expectations about concepts such as "responsibility," "cooperation," and "freedom."

Here is a general breakdown of the process: An experience happens. The mind kicks in and interprets it using thoughts and language. Sometimes this can be a useful survival skill, but more often than not we solidify our interpretations into beliefs and get stuck because we are always interpreting things through this filter.

As we grow more intimate with our mind states, we understand that these filters—these beliefs—are impermanent and subject to change. We do not identify with our thoughts and emotions, and recognize that they are just passing through. We begin to experience the linguistic component of thoughts, and how language both creates and conditions how we will ultimately experience things. Note the subtle difference between saying "I'm angry!" and "I'm experiencing anger right now!" In the first example, we identify ourselves as anger, in the second, there is the element of some distance. Note how often (and unmindfully) we say "I have to ..." instead of "I'm going to ..." or "I choose to ..." Do you see how the first choice of words limits your perception of freedom and self-direction? What would happen if you thought of going to work in a snowstorm as an adventure, rather than a great inconvenience or threatening situation?

Often the clear mind has been described as a pure bright sky, unobstructed by clouds. Our thoughts (and the reactive behavior patterns that result from them) cover up this radiant awareness. Sometimes the cloud cover is thin or sparse, but other times the sky is covered with raging storm clouds—thoughts that are confusing, or have enormous emotional impact. Mindful meditation helps us see the clouds for what they are: mental constructs. We can see clearly how certain beliefs limit us, how they constrict our perception, and that we can choose to let go of those beliefs and live with greater freedom. With the ability to see things clearly, the clouds gradually start thinning and eventually evaporate. This heralds the beginning of true wisdom. We begin to navigate our life with greater freedom and ease, and greater confidence in our ability to choose wisely.

EXERCISE 6: NAMING OUR THOUGHTS

Assume your preferred comfortable meditative posture, and focus on the breath in one of three areas: the nostrils, the heart center, or the navel. During meditation, if thoughts arise, simply name them (such as: thinking about the car inspection, thinking about dinner, thinking about the project at work, thinking about my son, etc.) and let them go. The practice here is simply noticing what thoughts arise, naming them, and then returning to the breath.

The Attitude of Loving-Kindness: Metta Meditation

The Pali word *metta* is commonly translated in English as "loving-kindness." Metta signifies friendship, nonviolence, and a strong intention for the happiness of others. Metta is in fact a very specific form of love—an attitude of caring for another independent of all self-interest. It sets forth a specific intention for human flourishing. Understandably, this attitude is often difficult to describe with words; however, in the practice of metta meditation, one recites specific words and phrases in order to evoke a "boundless warm-hearted feeling." The strength of this feeling is not limited to or by particular affiliations such as family, religion, or social class. It is a tool that permits one's generosity and kindness to be applied to all beings, and as a consequence, one finds true happiness in another person's happiness no matter who the individual is.

EXERCISE 7: PRACTICING METTA

The open-hearted work and repetition required of an individual engaged in metta practice endows the four universal wishes—to live happily, and to be free from hostility, affliction, and distress—with a very personal inner love. Within this practice is the power for personal transformation. If you are beginning metta practice, you may wish to start by offering these wishes for just ten to fifteen minutes each day. You may do your practice as a formal sitting meditation or while walking (preferably without destination). You may also choose to integrate your metta practice with daily chores.

To begin, take a few moments to quiet your mind, and focus your attention on the experience of loving kindness. You will begin by offering metta to someone you love. If distracting thoughts arise, acknowledge them and make a mental note to return to them afterwards, but quickly move them aside to maintain concentration.

First offer metta to someone you love, someone who has been important to you in your life, or someone who has helped you in some way. Call their image to mind, and open your heart as you recite the intentions to yourself:

- May s/he be well, happy, and at ease.

- May neither harm nor suffering come to him/her.

- May s/he be healthy and strong.

- May s/he have ease of well-being and fully accept all the conditions of the world.

Now that your heart is open, extend metta to yourself:

- May I be well, happy, and at ease.

- May no harm nor suffering come to me.

- May I be healthy and strong.

- May I have ease of well-being and fully accept all the conditions of the world.

Next, extend metta to a casual acquaintance or a neutral person, such as someone in your neighborhood you may recognize on sight, but do not know very well. Repeat the phrases in the first section for this individual.

The final step is to extend metta to a difficult person. It does not have to be for the most difficult person in your life, but could instead be someone you find presently difficult to be around. Please be aware that if doing so feels difficult or disingenuous at this time, skip this section for now. With continued practice, you will be able to greet even difficult people or those who behaved in a harmful way toward you with greater compassion. Once your metta flows easily, begin to include in your practice one or more of the following categories of people to whom you will offer it:

1. A close friend.

2. A neutral person (someone you neither like nor dislike).

3. A difficult person (no need to start with the *most* difficult person, but someone whom you have a distaste for).

4. All beings, individuals, personalities, and creatures. Choose whichever word to describe "all beings" that you please; it may be helpful to break up this category into subcategories: all men, and then all women, all beings who are happy, and then all beings who are both happy and suffering, and all beings who are primarily suffering.

Meditation in Daily Life

Whenever you are doing something, try to bring your full attention to the task. This may seem difficult in a busy work situation, but you can gradually train yourself to focus and shift your attention without regarding interruptions as distractions or pressures, but as opportunities to practice calmly shifting focus. Concentration helps us be more centered and focused. We enter the task without being distracted by thoughts of "liking" or "disliking," simply doing what needs to be done.

For practice, pick an activity and just focus on that, releasing all thoughts of past or future, or any idea of what is to be gained by doing it. In the doing, let there be just that, the doing. Even brushing your teeth mindfully adds a richer dimension to life. Showering, eating, cleaning, driving—essentially everything provides an opportunity for mindful entrance into the present.

Summary

Each type-specific chapter in this book is merely a summary of a much more involved meditation path. After practicing as suggested in this chapter, take a pause for reflection, and answer the following questions.

1. What stood out as significant for you in this chapter's practices?

2. Do you have any insight about why these were important for you? Do they relate to habitual patterns?

3. Note any other reasons why that certain exercise resonated with you.

4. Did this exercise help you becoming more aware of the interplay of thoughts and emotions?

5. What exercise felt right?

Use your intuition or gut reaction to this. Try to remove preconceived notions of which exercise you "should" practice or which exercise you may have tried earlier in your life.

Fifteen

·················

Type 6: Contemplative Inquiry

This most sophisticated form of meditation is also the simplest; paradoxical, yes, but that is the very nature of this type. The most profound meditation is a simple focus on one concept, which makes the simplest meditation profound! Conceptual meditation could be summed up as the meditation of no instruction, or at most, the meditation of one instruction. Whatever the specific topic of contemplative inquiry, you focus on just that one concept and meditate. Known as the "intellectual's form of meditation," the contemplation of one idea is an art honed by philosophers, inventers, and scientists as well as advanced meditators. However, like each of the paths in this book, familiarity with its specific teachings will assist you on your path.

The concentration-based meditation techniques where one thought is observed all share a similar definition in that the mind's attention gravitates to a single thought. What is not normally discussed is that thoughts may have varying degrees of simplicity. A concept or thought in the context of this discussion would have the least amount of intended density. The usual example of observing the breath is actually one of the denser presentations. You may go into the subtle levels of the breath in the enlightened state but you may also feel the physical experience of breathing. Similarly, you can view the visual image of a mantra, you can speak a mantra out loud, or you can contemplate the essence of the mantra. The basis of the concepts for contemplative inquiry is that there is very little to grasp.

Due to this level of subtlety, contemplative inquiry is also ripe for thought distractions, the biggest hurdle for people interested in this intellectual path. In the oral tradition of meditation, it is the brilliant, intellectual person who has the most difficult time simplifying the mind due to years of efforts at understanding profound truths. It is also understood that the person who has a sophisticated understanding of life on the one hand but who is able to remain simple, humble, and with warmth in their heart is the ultimate human being. The only difficulty is that reaching this state is not easy—so give yourself the appropriate amount of time! It is also the reason I do not force long meditation sessions on all people; for some, opening the heart may be more valuable to their lives than hours upon hours of silent contemplation.

Whether or not this form of meditation is for you, learn how the mind works when focusing on a concept. To highlight only a few select topics, the first exercise concerns self-inquiry. A cursory explanation of the Zen koan practice is applied in summary format to give a feeling of what I term "patient inquiry." The concept of *maya* or illusion is taught based on the great teacher Swami Vivekananda. A fourth exercise deals with St. Francis of Assisi and death of the ego.

As one develops in meditation, the form simplifies. Various literature may describe *the* meditation technique or *the* best teacher, but meditation only becomes more simple as you progress through committed practice. Each form is a thought itself. The subtle levels of meditation leave the form behind.

EXERCISE 1: RELAXATION ON EMPTINESS

Please try this exercise as a primer for contemplative inquiry. A small population of people interested in this type of meditation finds this relaxation exercise effective.

Sit or lie in a relaxed manner and unplug from technology for five to ten minutes. Imagine all the thoughts, pressures, stresses, and distractions leaving your mind in a slow and gradual manner. You feel a sense of peace in a state of emptiness. You may imagine an element of emptiness in your mind or a release in your heart. As soon as a thought enters, you go back to the physical feeling of relaxation surrounded by emptiness, of being enveloped in emptiness, filled with nothingness. Breathe in space, exhale space. Allow thoughts to pass and notice the tranquility that exists between thoughts. Notice everything drifting away into pure being.

Self-Inquiry Intro and Exercise

The great Indian saint Ramana Maharshi (1879–1950) had a profound awakening at age sixteen, shortly after the death of his father. Mystified by seeing his father's body without life, Ramana began contemplating the mystery of life. His device for understanding that caused his enlightenment is summed in asking the question "Who is the seer?" The context of life means that our mind sees something and makes sense of that thing or object of interest. If complete understanding of "Who is the seer?" in the mind is performed, there can be no words. The seer and the seen may be considered one and the same. When this happens, the once-separate ego is no longer separate and all inner strife disappears. This process sent Ramana Maharshi into years of complete spiritual absorption. His main method of teaching was having people stand in his presence to have to feel a sense of oneness.

When students asked for his counsel, his main teaching was that self-inquiry would provide a solution to all of the student's problems.

He promoted the practice of repeatedly asking the question, "Who am I?" It is very simple, but you may now have a chance to experiment with his practice.

EXERCISE 2: WHO AM I?

Begin by journaling your responses to the self-directed question "Who am I?" until you exhaust all of your perceived ego notions, such as: daughter, mother, friend, worker, parent, gardener, cook, cleaner, meditator, lover of movies, from this hometown, and so on and so forth. Go into explicit detail on this gross, outer level: I am the first daughter, I am a conflicted rebel, I am inquisitive and creative...Go on in more detail as you shed these outer layers: My best friend lives here. I, me, mine, my favorite [insert object here] is this, I used to like that, but now I like this...Keep going! Be borderline narcissistic until you realize that you are unique but not separate. Keep asking the question "Who am I?" See what emerges. What do you discover? After digging through the superficial layers, ask yourself "Who am I, *really?*" Continue asking until you again exhaust this level.

As you venture nearer to your true self, there is nothing more to report. You have summarized the contents of your ego. The question slows and so do the thoughts. When you feel as though the response to the "Who am I?" question is beyond words, you are deepening your meditation. If this exercise particularly resonates with you, I strongly encourage you look into the book *The Collected Works of Sri Ramana Maharshi,* edited by Arthur Osborne, for more information.

Zen Koans, or Intellectual Riddles

A strong emphasis in East Asian Buddhism is placed on breaking the mundane thinking patterns of the mind that misinterpret reality. These same thinking patterns also simply interpret reality when reality is too grand to be interpreted. A practice from the Zen tradition (*Ch'an* in Chinese), koan or paradoxical riddle was invented by the Master Hui-Neng (628-713 AD).

Hui-Neng believed in sudden enlightenment or the possibility that one may understand the essence of reality at any time. His rivals in that era believed in sitting in meditation for long hours before one could understand the mind. Hui-Neng achieved enlightenment in spite of his illiteracy. One day he heard a monk recite a Buddhist sutra and from that moment he left the marketplace to become a monk. His simple mindset allowed him the luxury of being free of the intellectual's complex understanding of reality.

Hui-Neng said:

> *If someone asks you about the primary meaning of life and he asks about "being," you answer "non-being." If he asks about "non-being," you answer "being." If he asks about "the common," you answer "the sage." If he asks about "the sage," you answer "the common." The two ways interact and produce the middle way. If all of your dialogues with other people follow this pattern, then you will not depart from the principle.*
> —(The Mind of Chinese Ch'an [Zen], Wu, 24–25)

Such an approach to discussions catches the listener by surprise—the mind is fooled by a response to a question in an unexpected manner. A deeply philosophical question may have its context in an academic setting, but when attempting to go beyond the thinking mind, simplicity is more efficient. However, a simple question may require some elaboration. Thus, when you face your own mind while meditating, treat yourself accordingly. Explore areas that you need to understand and let your intellect rest with the complicated questions, for example, after pondering an unanswerable question, such as "Why does human suffering exist?" While this question has responses, no definitive conclusion has been made over the course of thousands of years of discussion.

Another example are the traditional koans such as "What is the sound of one hand clapping?" An interesting koan in the form of a supposition from the Buddhist Heart Sutra: "Form is emptiness, emptiness is form."

A modern application to this practice is to ask a real life unanswerable question that stems from the human condition. For example, the existence of God has stumped humanity with the majority believing in God—yet not the atheist. This practice simply contemplates the question. However, if your back hurts and you wonder how to remedy the problem, ask concrete questions and address the situation. Or if you have little experience with meditation, ask questions and read books on the subject. Once you gain some experience, let go of your complex mind and attempt to be as simple as an empty vessel.

Koans take you beyond discursive thinking, and the answers can not be provided linguistically. "Working" a koan in your life means to examine a situation beyond concrete arguments or debates. You listen with all parts of your being; you exhaust all methods of inquiry. This process could extend for months or even years. You sit with the question and work on it. You are not out to prove a particular viewpoint but to break down your preconceived notions about reality. Again, if this concept resonates with you, there are numerous books written on Zen Koans. Resources include: *Zen Mind, Beginner's Mind* by Suzuki, *The Way of Zen* by Alan Watts, *Gateless Gate: The Classic Book of Zen Koans* by Koun Yamada, and *The Blue Cliff Record* by Thomas Cleary.

EXERCISE 3: REFLECTING ON AN
UNANSWERABLE QUESTION OR TOPIC
Examine a problem like violence, pollution, war, materialism, or another issue. Think deeply on this issue until you have no solution and attempt to go beyond the mind to find a mystical response. In the beginning of this practice you may research the topic to some degree before you feel as though you understand some existing arguments on the topic. Then

begin to use your intuition via meditation. At a certain point, the mind ceases to strive. Typical questions for meditative consideration are:

- "Why does war exist?"
- "Does God exist?"
- "What happens when a person dies?"
- "Why is there world hunger when there is enough food?"
- "Why does my friend have a disease at a young age?"

Feel free to create personally motivated questions.

Maya and the Concept of Illusion

The concept of *maya* (illusion) aims to reduce attachment to the mind's thoughts. Swami Vivekananda was one of the greatest teachers of the nondual Vedic philosophy. He was the first highly influential Indian to speak to Americans in his address to the 1893 World Parliament of Religions in Chicago. The force and clarity of Vivekananda's lecture surprised the world, as India was considered then to be a backwards country.

In his definition of the concept of maya, Vivekananda offers these words: "Because we talk in vain, and because we are satisfied with the things of the senses, and because we are running after desires; therefore, we, as it were, cover the Reality with a mist" (*Jnana Yoga*, 88). This mist is our ignorance. Reality itself is not an illusion, but our mind's limited perspective of reality is foggy. The purpose of meditation and mysticism is to clarify or clear the mind.

Vivekananda continues:

Thus we find that Maya is not a theory for the explanation of the world: it is simply a statement of facts as they exist, that the very basis of our being is contradiction, that everywhere we have to move through this tremendous contradiction, that wherever there is good, there must also be evil, and wherever there is evil, there

must be some good, wherever there is life, death must follow as
its shadow, and everyone who smiles will have to weep, and vice
versa. Nor can this state of things be remedied ... Thus the Vedanta
philosophy is neither optimistic nor pessimistic. It voices both these
views and takes things as they are.

—ibid, 97

As an aid to overcoming certain mental limitations in the process
of meditation, the idea that our mind is a limited tool can be helpful.
The mystics also state that as we become less attached to our individual
existence through our mind's perception, we become more able to experience reality fully.

Consciousness educator Christian de Quincey says:

All beliefs are limiting—because they are abstractions. Beliefs are
thoughts and concepts literally "abstracted" (taken from) the flow of
ongoing experience. They are snapshots of reality, frozen fragments
of consciousness. And because they are abstractions plucked from
the flow of experience, they can never connect us with reality. Both
reality and experience always happen now—right now.

Beliefs, on the other hand, are always and inevitably rooted in the
past. They come from experiences that have already have happened.
Much of the time these beliefs originated with other people, and are
filtered through a cultural framework. As long as we are focused on our
beliefs (even if we believe these beliefs are the truth) we miss the reality of what we are experiencing. In this sense, all beliefs are limiting to
some extent because they isolate us from what is real.

Even if this form of meditation is not the perfect fit for you, take
the essence of these teachings and examine how recognizing illusions in
your thought patterns holds back your level of meditation.

EXERCISE 4: RELAXATION BY REFLECTION ON ILLUSION

Each time you breathe in and out, notice your illusion or attachment to tension. Replace "My neck is tight" with "The neck area is tight" and then let it release with the breath. Notice that by disentangling from your physical body, you can decrease the ego's grip on the body and drift into a quiet relaxation. By letting go of the self-centered view of life, see how a relaxed experience broadens.

EXERCISE 5: REFLECTING ON SEEING ILLUSION IN YOUR THINKING

Reflect on these questions in your journal to begin this meditation exercise on illusion:

- What things keep you from doing your meditation?
- What are your material attachments?
- What desires cause you to be attached to your thoughts?

An example would be that I have to email all my friends on Facebook because they sent me messages, so I do not have extra time to meditate. My friends will be mad with me if I avoid them and I "want" them to like me. In the end, I think that I am a bad person if I do not fulfill my perceived understanding of what my friends need. I begin to realize that the person who has no time is living in an illusion. The short time used for meditation will help overcome the illusion that will ultimately bar a person from living into the fullness of his or her life.

EXERCISE 6: PRESENT MOMENT MEDITATION

Reflect on the concept of maya and discover some forms of thought that "mist" your understanding of the truth. Deep-seated desires and beliefs in our lives make us misperceive reality. When meditating on the concept of maya, aim for periods of silence in your mind. Whenever a thought arises, remind yourself that it is all an illusion. I want to especially point out how this exercise offers very little guidance compared to other meditation exercises in earlier chapters.

Egoless Meditation, or Surrendering the Ego

Monastic cultures throughout the world have practiced asceticism to gain spiritual wisdom. Modern religious practices include fasting, donating money to nonprofit causes, and giving up one's free time to serve the poor, in addition to a host of other disciplined activities. In the collective psyche, those who give up the material comforts are thought of as higher beings that are very close to the divine. Modern teachers have learned from the pious attitude of past spiritual leaders, yet often preach balanced living to curb the potentially unhealthy extremes of asceticism. One recent example is a man who fasted for forty days and forty nights and nearly died. His pious attempt at surrendering his ego resulted in his loved one's nursing him back to strength for three months. His efforts at egolessness ended up forcing others to take care of his ego and weak body.

The process of losing one's ego is an important step that the ascetic practitioners have correct. One of the most profound teachers of egolessness, St. Francis of Assisi, offers an example of how humility relates to meditation. One major difficulty with humility lies with self-esteem. Humility is an advanced attitude and unrelated to low self-esteem. The humble person has high self-esteem, therefore they need no adoration. Using the Pure Thinking philosophy from chapter 5, as a paradigm for psychological states the negative thinking pattern is low self-esteem. One who does not value his or her own standing may appear to be humble by placing others above them. However, this low self-esteem is actually a depressed state. The positive phase of the triad would be the egocentric person who over values his or her own needs. Alternatively, the pure-minded person understands they are not the center of reality, but has high self-worth.

St. Francis discusses the theme of "dying to the self" in order to know a reality higher than normal waking consciousness. He thanks people who persecute him for he agrees that his ego is not very valuable in the larger context of the universe. If St. Francis trusts his limited personal mind in his profound contemplation, he will be deluding himself versus centering on a reality larger than his own mind. St. Francis has no low self-esteem—he created a religious order that continues to this day. St. Francis has a healthy self-esteem because he relies on the higher wisdom to which his own human mind surrenders.

The Prayer of St. Francis

Lord, make me an instrument of thy peace. Where there is hatred, let me sow love; where there is injury, pardon; where there is doubt, faith; where there is despair, hope; where there is darkness, light; where there is sadness, joy.

O divine Master, grant that I may not so much seek to be consoled as to console, to be understood as to understand, to be loved as to love; For it is in giving that we receive; it is in pardoning that we are pardoned; It is in dying [to self] that we are born to eternal life.

The final statement of St. Francis's prayer is his teaching of humility. He figuratively applies the image of death to the human ego. This equates meditation's approach to cessation of the thoughts of the mind. The purpose of meditation is to focus the mind, allowing the normal mind chatter to cease and allowing the light of a higher reality to shine in a person's being. St. Francis discusses being "reborn" as the more enlightened state, and thus as being reborn to eternal life. Remember that the new rebirth was not a sacrifice but a letting go of a lower state of being that leaves you feeling an "eternal" peace.

EXERCISE 7: RELAXATION VIA MERGING WITH THE UNIVERSE

As you inhale and exhale in a comfortable relaxation posture, reflect on the fact that your breath is the universe's breath. As you inhale receive the larger universe; as you exhale, release into that universe. Begin to release the tension that represents a separation from that larger universe. Continue with this process that prepares you for meditation.

EXERCISE 8: PRACTICING HUMILITY

As a second exercise, notice how the prayer of St. Francis relates to your life. In a journal, note existing areas in your life where humility plays a role. Is there an area of difficulty where you may use the formula of "death and rebirth" of developing self-esteem through mystical reflection? Take some time to think deeply and determine how humility can enrich your life. St. Francis spent hours upon hours during his retreats in deep contemplation, much of which was related to his developing an understanding of humility. Meditate on your own insights in a similar, dedicated manner.

EXERCISE 9: MERGE YOUR CONSCIOUSNESS WITH THE SAINT

Spend some time studying the St. Francis prayer and reflect on it. Can you use your intuition to feel how it would be to have a conversation with the saint? Attempting to understand the inspired mind of spiritual writers is a good method of scripture study and key practice of contemplative inquiry.

Summary

Each type-specific chapter in this book is merely a summary of a much more involved meditation path. After practicing as suggested in this chapter, pause for reflection and answer the following questions.

1. What stood out as significant for you in this chapter's practices?

2. Do you have any insight about why these were important for you? Do they relate to habitual patterns?

3. Note any other reasons why that certain exercise resonated with you.

4. Did this exercise help you becoming more aware of the interplay of thoughts and emotions?

5. What exercise felt right?

Use your intuition or gut reaction to this. Try to remove preconceived notions of which exercise you "should" practice or which exercise you may have tried earlier in your life.

Part IV

Sustaining a
Meditation
Practice

What does it take to sustain a meditation practice? As much as we may want the benefits meditation brings, we inevitably face the resistance of our ingrained habits of thought and emotion. The key is to remember that meditation is a **process,** and that meditators are not perfect people with perfect thoughts, emotions, and behaviors. The top ten reasons people struggle with meditation and how these struggles relate to yoga's time-honored precepts for living well are explored. In addition to identifying these issues, readers are encouraged to join a meditation group for support.

Part IV's Rationale

In organizing a course for those who have taken to meditation, I noticed that the first two steps in yoga's eightfold path to meditation outline five principles that cause resistance to meditation practice and five principles that support meditation practice. The ten short chapters of part IV target common struggles that students have raised in group discussions.

Five Behaviors to Restrain

- Chapter 16: Doing No Harm
- Chapter 17: Living in Truth
- Chapter 18: What "Non-Stealing" Entails
- Chapter 19: Freedom in Self-Restraint
- Chapter 20: Freedom from Greed

Five Behaviors to Observe

- Chapter 21: Balance and Perspective
- Chapter 22: Contentment
- Chapter 23: The Value of Discipline
- Chapter 24: Self-Study
- Chapter 25: The Meaning of Surrender

Benefiting from Part IV's Exercises

As there are ten chapters in part IV, each with various thought-provoking exercises, please read through the various chapters and perform only the reflection exercises that connect to your questions or needs. Concentrate your energy on the exercises that help you now. If you are newer to meditation, the entirety of part IV may be of interest to you in the future, once you begin to traverse meditation's inner journey. While some introspection serves you in meditation practice, less can be more—especially when you need time to breathe, relax, and meditate!

Sixteen

Doing No Harm

Facing the Shadow from the Past

While timing is unique and unpredictable, meditation training taps each participant's psyche at a deep level. As soon as the mind quiets, like the water of the still pond, deeper issues become exposed. Positive feelings like joy and peacefulness appear in stronger states. Corresponding difficult feelings like sadness or other painful mentalities may surprise the meditator who seeks peace. While each one of us must journey through the vicissitudes of life, at least we can expect these emotional responses to meditation.

Balance with these emotions is one goal. It is fine to continue laughing and feeling the normal range of emotions, for learning from the emotions and issues that arise defines the meditative mind. The meditation practitioner aims to be perfect in learning but not perfect in life. Journaling and discussing personal issues with trusted friends can be healing. Please be aware, however, that there are times that deep-seated unresolved issues may require a professional counselor to resolve.

Be careful of emotional projection that may occur unexpectedly. Projection means applying or blaming a personal inner state of mind to an unrelated subject or person. If you find yourself having strong emotional reactions to your instructor or a classmate, please discreetly discuss this with the instructor.

Another sign of overwhelming emotions is expressed as an avoidance of one's personal meditation practice. At this point, you are advised to discuss this with the class or your instructor. Taking time to journal or process the emotion may be the appropriate response. Be careful not to think that meditation is the cause of the emotional state; meditation can be the vehicle that allows deep inner healing.

If your meditation practice continues to feel overwhelming, you may need to adjust your approach. The safest way to adjust is to practice exercises from the chapters of part II: Do more deep breathing and relaxation exercises, or work on your five senses to cultivate inner stillness. The exercises in part II also quiet the mind but may be a better fit if silent meditation is giving you trouble.

Nonviolence and the Past

For most human beings, the present means the summation of the past up to this present moment. Human interactions are based on the associations from our previous experiences. This ability to remember the past gives the human mind a distinct skill in the animal kingdom. This ability, however, can also lock us into a reality from the past that may not exist in the present moment. In other words, the mind is constantly biasing reality based on past experiences. Unresolved past experiences are especially problematic.

Once upon a time, a young man whose family was overbearing moved far away from his homeland in search of inner peace. Not soon thereafter, the young man was promoted in his new job and met a new boss who physically resembled the father he left behind. Needless to say, the young man could not see his boss as the kind person he was nor could he hear his kind instructions. He relived his past and kept seeing his father in the new boss. The young man was stuck in the unsolved past that was brought up by the new "father figure." At night when the young man sat to perform his meditation practice, he started to think about his day at work as well as his childhood. His meditation was not about the present moment; it was rooted in the past.

This example is normal for meditation practitioners. The same human mind that collects wisdom from past experiences also holds onto past issues. If you have a major past trauma, it is important to work with a counselor who specializes in healing that type of trauma. However, if you simply have memories of events not considered traumas, you still have emotions that linger in your mind. Meditation practice brings these events to the forefront of your mind. In the quiet of the still pond, the depths are revealed.

This example relates to unresolved emotions. Most of us have many of these "unresolutions" that reveal their existence when we react strongly to situations. The practice does not remove these memories from our mind as brainwashing might attempt. The point is to understand, accept, and ultimately release the associated emotion. For example, if our young man can understand his feelings about his father, he will retain the memories but not the negative charge. This will give our young man wisdom in the place where pain existed.

Remember that meditation is only one process for self-realization, a term for the pursuit of spiritually aware living or for deep happiness. There are many processes for self-realization, from personal growth movements to religious practice. The techniques, while important, are secondary to personal growth. In the case of many personal-growth activities, there is a tendency to fantasize that the technique will do all the work and magically remove life's challenges. In this case, a person relies on following a meditation technique as if the technique will make the change. The technique serves as a mirror for self-understanding. It is self-understanding that leads to self-realization.

EXERCISE 1: SELF-AWARENESS—
MOVE FORWARD BY FIRST KNOWING WHERE YOU ARE
In your journal, list one to three examples of healed past experiences. For example, our young man earlier decided to work on viewing his new boss as an individual instead of a version of his father. Each time he had an adverse reaction to his boss, he learned from that feeling. He used the distance from his real father to understand his childhood. He went so far as entrusting his boss with this information, and he became an ally in the young man's personal process. The boss was extraordinary, and in time, the young man learned to accept his father as well as his own reactions. While not completely resolved, the young man's meditation was no longer disturbed by unsettling thoughts after six months of practice.

As you list and work through a few situations you have overcome in your life, notice your own process of understanding the event, accepting it, and eventually releasing it to live in the present. Learn from your success and insights.

The next step is to list in your journal one to three examples of disturbing past experiences. You may choose a simple stressor like traffic or a mundane task you dread on a daily basis. Or, you may choose a more complex interpersonal situation you dwell upon when you sit in meditation. This list may be long, including childhood situations, interactions from high school, health issues, financial troubles, and so forth. Choose just one situation as your object for meditation practice one week.

Apply the concept of nonviolence to this situation in the form of acceptance, love, compassion, or forgiveness. Hold onto that version of nonviolence. At first, journaling may be the most valuable form of reflection on the issue. Then, sit quietly and allow your mind to focus on this topic from a spiritual perspective. Each individual may accomplish this exercise in his or her own manner, be it visual, intellectual, prayerful, in the form of light, as a mantra, or another related approach. The point is that you are gaining personal insights into the situation so that you are able to find a sense of self-realization.

EXERCISE 2: RELAXATION OF LETTING GO (FROM CHAPTER 7)

Recline in a comfortable position. Imagine floating on a river. You float very safely and can feel the gentle current of the water drifting peacefully. Beside you, a basket floats where you may place any worries, concerns, or issues that weigh on your mind. You will take a break from these issues as you mentally place them in the basket.

Continue breathing and floating as you feel tensions release with each exhalation.

When new issues arise, place those in this basket too. Allow yourself to temporarily let go of past hurts, regrets, and resentments. As you place these issues in the basket, notice how you feel and remain passively aware.

Continue breathing and floating continuing to feel a deeper state of relaxation.

At the end of the relaxation, your perception will alter slightly, helping you understand the issues in the basket from a new perspective. You neither denied these issues nor dwelled on them; you allowed a sense of acceptance of life to soothe the body and mind with relaxation.

Seventeen

Living in Truth

Proper Speech and Inner Dialogue

Paula Green's book *Reconciliation and Forgiveness in Divided Societies: A Path of Courage, Compassion, and Commitment* recounts an amazing story of a group of Tibetan monks who remained compassionate toward their torturers. Held by Chinese captors, the monks felt compassion for the soldiers who were ordered to torture the prisoners. The famed monk Lopon never gave into negative feelings. Instead, he interpreted the actions from a compassionate perspective. A believer in reincarnation of the soul, he felt sorry for the future lives of the Chinese soldiers. Lopon's worldview includes a strong belief in the concept of karma that encompasses future lives for the soul based on present life actions. Lopon also knew that his own karma would be adversely affected were he to curse his captures—in his eyes it would be no different that bringing hatred into his present and future.

This extreme example explains how negative thoughts are one of the main reasons for avoiding personal meditation practice as well as performing meditation incorrectly. If one of us has a negative thought about another person—something that may occur on a daily basis—that thought is turned inward while meditating. While sitting still, no one is to blame for our negative thoughts or unhappy feelings. The meditation practitioner is left to his or herself in those moments. If those negative thoughts are not framed in a positive fashion, meditation will be very, very tiresome, uncomfortable, and even unbearable.

Fortunately, the example of Lopon and his monks gives us the inspiration to handle lesser negative thoughts. This message helps ask the question "What is the truth in this situation?" Each situation in life is interpreted by the human being. Individuals are named "individuals" because they each have a different response to a situation. The response to torture for most of us is disgust or anger toward the person inflicting the pain. However, Lopon shows that compassion may be another response to the situation. By his willpower, Lopon was able to transform a situation.

While we may not know Lopon's internal process, we can be certain that for most people who overcome a difficult situation, there was an internal process at work to reach that deeper truth of compassion. This process may never end as the human mind continually finds reasons to be agitated, which is why the term "unconscious" has retained its relevance. Each of us sitting here has unconscious issues at play at all times. Here are a few clues to our mind's operation. These types of reactions occur in the midst of daily life and are very revealing.

Remember that our culture commonly assumes that external divisions remain external. For example, Mr. X was rude on the other side of the room as he mindlessly yelled at people. However, as soon as Mr. Y. thinks "There goes Mr. X again. He is a mean person," Mr. Y has internalized the same negative state. If Mr. Y. sees Mr. X's rudeness with compassion, then Mr. Y remains in a peaceful state of mind. Mr. Y thinks, "I feel compassion for Mr. X, who has to keep yelling to get his point across."

The internal effect on our minds is what is at stake here and the following exercise may help with remedying these issues.

EXERCISE 1: THE PRACTICE OF
LOOKING THROUGH THE LENS OF VIRTUE

Determine one virtue that holds power for you and simply hold that virtue in your mind. Compassion is a good example (especially in light of this chapter), however virtues akin to love, joy, acceptance, peace, faith, and others work just as well depending on your situation. This practice holds the virtue in the mind and lets that virtue be the lens for an interpretation of a situation that occurs in your mind. View your own thoughts in terms of virtue. Practice this exercise briefly in the morning as a reminder to handle daily events with this truthful approach. In the evening, review events of the day from this truth lens and reframe any disturbing situations.

If a persistent thought keeps appearing in your meditation, begin to work with the roots of that thought in a journal or in a method that helps you gain a deeper understanding of the unconscious thought or feeling. As you make progress with these disturbances, you will be able to reengage the mind quieting. Without facing these issues, meditation can turn into a self-defense mechanism.

1. Notice your first reaction to a situation. Be careful to learn the roots of your reaction versus simply replacing the reaction with a positive.

2. Reflect on alternate responses to the situation through the lens of your chosen virtue.

3. Hold onto the virtue each time that you reflect on that situation.

4. Remember that these steps are for your internal mind's peacefulness. You then determine your actions as you see fit for the situation. You may still reprimand a child, but you would

express boundaries or punishments with love. You may still discuss an unjust situation with a coworker, only you will do so with compassion.

EXERCISE 2: REFLECTION MEDITATION OR JOURNALING

Observe life from a spiritually based perspective akin to compassion or your virtue of choice. Treat your own internal thoughts in the same manner and notice how you may remain unaffected by a stressful life situation while meditating without ignoring that situation. Try to practice at least a few minutes twice per day, even if one of the sessions is only for a few minutes.

Eighteen

What "Non-Stealing" Entails

Listening to Emotions

Theft in real life happens rarely, if you think of the number of times that your car is not stolen, the number of times that the cashier gives you the correct change, and about a million other social interactions throughout your day. However, if you look into more subtle levels of theft, we are every one of us taking from nature, often without appreciation. We love things that are "free," but is it possible for anything to *really* have no cost attached? Think about more subtle forms of stealing, and think of stealing others' time, or think of stealing your own time. By not listening to others and yourself, all of us are hijacking our lives by missing out on life's subtle joys and realities. Here are some often overlooked examples, as stealing occurs in so many subtle ways in modern society:

1. Overstimulation via technology, cable television, Internet, cell phones, and the like do not allow processing time for normal life events. Technological living steals from quiet time.

2. Conversations where both parties are thinking about their next words, not listening to the other person perpetuates a double theft. First, we steal from the other person by not listening attentively. Secondly, we steal from ourselves by not appreciating that person.

3. We steal from our own quiet time by filling it with endless activities; hence we do not process our emotions.

EXERCISE 1: SINCERE LISTENING

When in a conversation, see if you can only listen to and ask questions of a friend without interjecting any of your own opinions.

1. Ask your friend to describe one type of stress that interferes with tranquility of mind.

2. The listeners have to understand that they have never had a similar situation, so refrain from making comments that assume understanding. Just Listen. A common response is "Oh, I've had that..." However, you have never had their pain because you are not the same person with the same kind of stress, and you do not know why the person had that particular pain.

3. Ask about the emotion the speaker felt from the stress, and steer the speaker to speak only about his/her feelings and not to blame the situation for the feeling. For example, the speaker says: "The traffic really bothers me. I hate these aggressive drivers." One response you could provide is: "What emotion do you feel?" Then, the speaker might avoid feeling the emotion by saying, "You know how it is, there are just too many cars on the road these days. It is really stressful." A speaker in touch with his or her feelings may say, "I felt annoyed because I feel pressure to be at work on time."

4. The final step is to resolve the emotion versus bleeding into a state of complaining. An emotion is processed when it is understood. The emotion changes immediately due to integration of the situation within the speaker. If the speaker repeats the example over and over, then no internal processing has occurred and a state of complaining ensues. Try to move into peace by the end of the exercise.

Whenever a person speaks in terms of emotional avoidance, there is a suppression of feelings that occurs. As this pattern builds, years of unresolved emotions store in the psyche. As more and more gets tucked away, the person begins to feel these stored emotions each time they sit to meditate. Many times, meditation is associated with emotional turmoil as if the meditation caused the emotions.

By listening to your emotions on a daily basis, you can understand the roots of your thinking and have the tools to release those issues. In time the emotions quiet, and the meditation offers glimmers of profound inner peace.

Exercise 2: Review the Day

In your journal (or mentally, if that is more your style) spend some time to review your day without any emotional reaction. Simply spend five minutes remembering each act you performed from waking to the end of the day. If you perform the exercise in the evening, begin with that morning. If you perform this exercise in the morning, trace the previous twenty-four hours.

For example:

I woke up early at 3:30 a.m. and closed the window, I drank some water. A truck drove by. I fell back asleep until 6:30 a.m. I woke, got up, and accidentally tapped the scale and the scale's light turned on. I dressed and went downstairs. Then, as I went to make some lemon water, I noticed the counter was jammed with last night's dishes. I wondered why those dishes were not washed…At 6:45 a.m. I had my first emotional reaction. In my mind, I drifted into an emotional state as I chose to feel inconvenienced by last night's dishes…

Continue with the exercise throughout the entire day. The goal is to learn how emotional you are throughout the day and how you view the fluctuations of your mind. You may notice one time during the day where you start to think more about the emotion than about the actual actions. Take a moment to understand those emotions. As the emotions are understood, you will recognize that the charge or disturbance drops away. This exercise helps you bridge the gap between the meditative state of mind while sitting quietly and the meditative state of mind while in the midst of an active day.

As you reclaim meaning from life, you will start to feel very content. In fact, as you figure out how not to steal from your own experience of life, fulfillment blossoms. While your bank account may or may not increase, you will feel very wealthy in spirit.

Nineteen

Freedom in Self-Restraint

Moderation of Desiring Fame and Power

Brahmacarya, the original Sanskrit term, may be translated loosely as moderation. Technically, this yogic virtue is defined as *carya*—being a student—of *Brahman*, or the absolute reality. This term is classically defined as chastity; a modern interpretation for the householder is moderation. For our application to meditation, the goal is to understand that materialistic desires may fuel excessive living. Desires after pleasure relate to this topic. This discussion focuses particularly on the desires for power and fame. While these may not appear to be pleasures, these issues lie beneath most pleasurable distractions. Any seasoned meditation practitioner knows the strength of desires for creating non-stop thought disturbances that cause avoidance to meditation at the worst and a scattered mind at the best.

The "I want" statement summarizes the bane of desire-based meditation disturbances. The desire-based thoughts fuel a host of disturbances and are very important to understand throughout the meditation practice. There are many levels as well as many categories of desire.

Desire for Power

With the technological advances brought by Western civilization, human living standards of health and convenience have temporarily improved. Outwardly, we have clean water and temperature-controlled homes, but the planet's ecological balance is paying the price. In its abundance of convenience, modern living has thoroughly skewed our sense of moderation. Imagine telling a child he or she is not allowed to use the Internet, television, iPods, cell phones, or electronic toys. Tell an adult he or she must turn off the air conditioner in summer or forgo driving a car. These conveniences are not necessary for healthy living, but over time the conveniences become the norm. Turn back the clock to 1960: few people had air conditioners and the home computer did not exist—interestingly and perhaps ironically, there was less talk of stress years ago.

These modern comforts allow a person the illusion of control over life: turn on the spigot, and the water flows at your command. From these creature comforts, humans may mistakenly feel powerful. This addiction to comfort is an expression of a feeling of power or control. The need for power is not necessarily over another human being but over our own fears. The truth of the matter is that the human being has no control over nature, and the sense of power is a complete illusion. Therefore, to the degree that we allow the perspective of human being over nature, the stronger the thought disturbances become. Any illusion regarding reality creates multiple thoughts in the mind and leads to instability.

As soon as "I want" to control life, I think—and I think a lot—about what "I want." Even a young child who says, "I want" this or that can manipulate an entire room of adults. The human will grab onto the desire and presses incessantly. However, the fact that stress is on the rise proves the point that no amount of (perceived) control over reality will bring peace of mind. The increase in the number of daily thoughts associated with modern appliances is an active contributor to low quality of inner-life that leads to stress. The stress, in turn, creates new health concerns that technology was trying to solve in the first place. Remember, technology's original mission was to improve health and happiness, not create more distress.

Exercise 1: Personal Reflection on "Power over Life"

1. Make an honest list of things that you would like to control. Some examples may be:

   a. I would like to end world hunger, war, and domestic violence.

   b. I would like to eliminate diseases from the world.

   c. I want to fix broken hearts.

   d. I want to steer my company in a "green" and profitable direction.

   e. I want my kids to learn meditation!

   f. I want to retire early; I do not want to work past sixty years of age.

2. Write the positive reasons for your desire for control.

   a. I do not want to see people suffer (I do not want to suffer).

   b. I do not want anyone to be sick, especially not those I love.

   Continue with your "honest" reasons.

3. Write why that is unrealistic as there is really no control over these aspects of nature.

Remember, not even the world's leaders are able to fix the world-wide hunger issue, let alone me as one person. The same thing is true with scientists of the world; as soon as one disease is managed, a new epidemic appears on the horizon.

4. Figure out a plan to accept your positive wishes while releasing the need for control at the same time.

EXERCISE 2: UNPLUG YOURSELF FROM TECHNOLOGY

A second exercise helps to understand your relationship to "power" or control over nature. Attempt to unplug yourself from technology for a few days—so long as you are not hurting others nor risking losing your job. Please refrain from using the radio in the car, using the Internet or computer outside of work, and the TV or other electronic entertainment devices at home for a few days. Essentially, "go Amish"; live as if you were born in the pre-electronic age as much as possible for a few days, and see how it affects your thoughts.

An amusing anecdote was the country rancher who had a demand from stressed-out city slickers to vacation on his ranch to work the farm. The rancher was laughing aloud when the wealthy professionals paid top dollar to be able to clean his stables—shoveling manure included free of charge!

Desire for Fame

Once you have learned to balance the desire for comforts, the next step surrounds the larger concept named fame. Normally, only movie stars and other national figures might be considered famous. However, recognition for good deeds at work is a type of fame-seeking. Try noticing a time in your life when someone did not recognize you and how much time you may have spent agonizing over the lack of fame (recognition). This doesn't mean we can't honor others or receive praise gracefully. The question remains: How is the mind affected by what others think of us?

A good solution for this is to realize that we only need to be "famous" or respected by ourselves.

A second area of fame has to do with your reputation. Depending on your personality type, some people like to be respected. Others value their friends and want to be liked by others. A third example is people who find harmony from family members as their version of fame. The intensity of these types of thoughts is enough to keep one from meditation or at the least is disrupting.

Exercise 3: Practicing Recognition

Take a moment and write down the names of three people you wish would openly praise and honor you. It could be a boss from the past, a teacher, or an adult in your life who treats you poorly, for example. Imagine if each of these people gave you the respect you feel you deserve. Write down what they would say. Now, notice how you feel thereafter. In as precise terms as possible, explain how you feel. In your own mind, you have just given yourself the respect you need. See if you can internalize the words that would have been said to you. In other words, if the boss would say, "Good job," then say "Good job" to yourself. With this self-recognition, notice how *you* feel and retain that no matter what others may think about you or say (or not say) to you. Continue doing this exercise; you will realize that *you* are the only person who makes you famous in your heart. After years of practice and cultivation of these ideas, desires lessen and the mind eventually transforms into one focused on higher consciousness or spiritual principles.

Exercise 4: Meditation Practice

The goal of this meditation exercise is to give yourself the wholeness you already possess but may not receive. Sit comfortably and focus on a light in your heart. Allow this light in your heart to symbolize a feeling of completeness. By accepting that you do not control the universe, you become strong in the truth. You are whole in just being who you are at this stage of your life. In other words, open yourself up to being fully present.

Twenty

Freedom from Greed

Abolishing Desires for More

The amount of thought distractions generated by human desires directly occupies two short chapters but indirectly relates to hundreds of situations in your daily life. In terms of material items, the usage of possessions serves us in the moment. However, the amount of time cleaning, caring, buying, paying off, locking, attaching to, dreaming about, and remembering those same possessions creates an inordinate number of thought disturbances. This is known as being "possessed by possessions" or as "possessive possessions." In other words, the human mind may be overly concerned with material items.

Meditation theory teaches that the human mind lacks stability. The slightest event can wreak havoc on emotions and thoughts. Because change is one of nature's constants, the mind is constantly pushed in many directions. The change from morning to night is normal; no one has an emotional crisis when the sun sets. In our wisdom, we understand that the sun sets each evening and that time is moving perpetually.

The psyche starts to disconnect from wisdom when our earthly possessions change like the night to day. Look around your home and recognize that all—yes, a hundred percent—of the items in the room have changed in the past year. Everything is a year older; even your hundred-year-old desk is now one year creakier. The mind does not accept that every possession is changing, so we become mired in attachments to things remaining constant. Hence we worry as our concerns lead to a state of possession by possessions.

Due to the power of the mind's desire to possession of things, many monastic traditions include a vow of poverty. Poverty could be defined as "nonpossessiveness of material items." This vow serves as a reminder that the material world is in fact temporal and that a more divine consciousness exists.

A secondary and more insidious type of thought generated by the desire for things is the fantasy or dream of having something that you do not yet own. Now the irony in this illusion is that ownership of material items is an impossibility in the first place. So, if I follow the American dream of having my own home, car, and all those technological devices, then my dream is a double illusion. First of all, dreaming disregards the present joy that exists right now. And secondly, ownership is impossible. This may sound strange and is not the way our culture operates, but stay with the discussion just a little longer.

Dreaming of future happiness based on having a thing causes us to forget that happiness is derived from a spiritual perspective that exists in the here and now. Meditating quietly brings inner peace. Just ask any billionaire if he or she is happy and they will say that money cannot buy you happiness; and recall that the happiest billionaires give away the majority of their money to charity.

Ownership is a human concept to keep material items organized in human society. In order to make sure that each person reaches work on time, our society assigns a car to individuals by offering ownership. This permits the car owner to wash, register, maintain, and drive the car. In reality, owning a car means caring for a car. The owner of the car pays for the luxury of quick travel with money and time. Think of your possessions as extended family whom you care for. See how much thought, time, energy, and money goes into living the materially wealthy life. If you are not wealthy enough to have a butler, driver, maid, cook, and personal attendant, imagine the amount of time involved in training, consoling, disciplining, and hiring new employees demands—you might even need a manager for all of your caretakers who oversee all of your possessions!

Exercise 1: Releasing Possession's Possession of Your Mind

1. Write down a list of your major possessions.

2. Notice which of these possessions are necessary and which are luxury items. Keep in mind that almost all possessions are a luxury, such as a car, TV, hot water, running water, phone … you get the idea. Nonluxury possessions are food, clothing, housing, and things essential to basic survival.

3. Examine each possession in cost, time, cleaning, security, and other concerns. For example: An automobile costs some amount. I clean it twice a month. I get a repair and oil change four times a year. I pay insurance. I take the time to lock it and have concerns for theft. I feel some emotion when it breaks down. See where this is going?

4. As a reality check, devise a new way of relating to your temporary possessions. Examine if you should buy more or let go of possessions, or downgrade to less expensive versions. Remember that the possession is not really yours and that you are only caring for the temporary item.

5. Experience peace of mind on the level of possessions.

EXERCISE 2: REMOVING HAPPINESS
FROM DREAMING OF FUTURE POSSESSIONS

1. Make a list of things that you want in your future. Things like a new home, car, boat, a secure early retirement plan, or a fancy wedding are all quite common and perfect for this exercise.

2. Notice how the capitalistic culture promotes materialism down to lectures given by popular gurus on achieving material wealth. Understand how these thoughts were ingrained in your thinking.

3. Rewrite your goals with "peace of mind" at the top followed by other rational plans, and that further material goals must fall in line with the "peace of mind" step.

4. Sit quietly with a sense of freedom from the "happiness" of material items.

Comfort with Silence

When the above exercise reaches a deep level in the consciousness and the attachment for desires lessens, moments of silence may occur. While there may be possessions around, when the attachment to these possessions drops away, silence prevails. These items may be cleaned after meditation practice. Cultivation of mind takes precedence over the rush of materialism. The silence offers no outward sign of success, and there are no inward fireworks or applause. There is silence. This following meditation practice fosters a communion with silence.

EXERCISE 3: MEDITATION PRACTICE OF COMFORT WITH SILENCE

Building on the practice of reducing and even "fasting" from external stimulation and entertainment from technology, learn to feel comfortable with silence. Take time each day to be quiet. Sit quietly as a meditative practice. Do not have any preset intention or agenda for the practice; just see how you respond to the silence. If you are newer to meditation practices, notice how your feel and how silence is not part of modern life. If your mind is trying to play tricks on you by overthinking or feeling that sitting still is a waste of time, perform some of the journaling exercises from this and previous and chapters. Please perform these exercises with no background music or other stimulus. For more advanced practitioners, notice how you respond to deeper levels of silence where no thoughts are present. Have you ever reached a state of "one thought," and could you remain in that level of inner silence?

Twenty-One

Balance and Perspctive

Purity of Mind Through Effort and Detachment

If the mind is vibrating at a high beta-wave state that produces feelings of stress and anxiety, there is a natural desire to move into the peaceful alpha state as soon as possible. In some situations, a person may turn to various drugs to induce temporary relief. Other unhealthy coping mechanisms are well-known in the field of addictions, such as eating, overworking, or other sensory stimulating activity.

Meditation as a possible solution introduces newfound hope. Ironically, the expectations interpreted from books on meditation or from mass media claim that meditation leads from stress to peace very quickly. The first part of the previous statement is factual: meditation does lead toward peace. And it is true, when the mind reaches a deep alpha or theta brain-wave state, a profound sense of peacefulness ensues. In these deeper states of mind, the meditation practitioner may feel at peace in the midst of a broken world. Often omitted from the magazine articles that tout studies performed on Tibetan monks' minds during deep trances is mention of the long and arduous trail one must walk to reach those profound experiences.

Problem 1: There is no way to understand a state of consciousness that has yet to be experienced. Therefore, it is difficult to know what type of practice is best suited to reach that state.

Solution 1: The way to reach this pure state is to proceed one step at a time. There is no skipping of steps. What can help you in this process is to realize that inner peace exists at all times and that there is peace in life at all times. The human mind is what is full of illusion. Eventually, this human mind can be made fit to understand the profound peace of life by methodical purification. As thoughts are measured by frequencies, you may learn to match the appropriate meditative exercise that will help balance your thought waves. These waves change from day to day. A meditation session may begin with gentle stretching, relaxation, and breathing in order to move the mind into a quieter frequency (as illustrated in part II of this book) prior to attempting meditation. Over time, you will learn the type of routine that works for your mind.

Problem 2: If you try too hard, thought disturbances are created. If you do not try hard enough, thought disturbances are created. A balance between effort and detachment must be struck.

Solution 2: Balance the effort with detachment, which means keeping a daily practice and giving yourself years to measure progress. Many of us use an external motivator to force us to maintain peace and we try very hard for a limited amount of time; when the external stressor abates, the impetus for meditation ceases. Try to allow the effort to be moderate and consistent over the long term. If you miss a day, it is OK, restart the next day.

Problem 3: Our society continues to send messages that happiness is a right which contradicts the amount of patience required for successful meditation.

Solution 3: If your goal is very concrete, like achieving something from meditation, then your meditation is pressured to attain the goal. Work on shifting the goal oriented thinking from "goal" to "direction." As you have a direction to head in life, then you are always on the path, literally and figuratively. Use the direction as motivation to continue the meditation journey. Make inner peace a directional signpost and be pleased with steps toward that signpost. This way, you will not set up an all-or-nothing scenario where you succeed or fail. When this happens in meditation, the trend is to give up at worst case or say "Meditation doesn't work." It works over the long term—the "long term" that is the rest of your life.

Problem 4: Once deeper states have been experienced, and you learn that the states are always changing, you may feel like you are finished with meditation or no longer need to put forth any effort as you have progressed. Apathy or arrogance sets in.

Solution 4: Being in a meditation or spiritual community supports the journey of understanding the sublime balance between effort and detachment. In other words, being with others serves as a reminder that the path is the destination. If you do feel that meditation exercises are becoming rudimentary, begin teaching others; it may awaken your "beginner's mind."

EXERCISE 1: UNDERSTANDING EXPECTATION

Be especially honest with the responses to these questions. Try to discover what you really think. You may know the correct answers intellectually, but try to write your more self-centered answers so that you can understand what would block you from a lifelong practice of meditation.

By realizing your preconceived expectations, you have the chance to alter those expectations.

Start by listing your personal expectations of meditation.

1. What do you think meditation practice will give you?

2. How long will it take you to gain these?

3. How would you realign these expectations?

List what you think are your impurities or disturbances with your meditation practice.

1. What are your weak thought patterns?

2. What are your gifts and strengths in living a meditative lifestyle?

List how you will be both active and patient with your disturbances.

1. How do you accept yourself for not being a perfect meditator?

2. How do you remain balanced between the effort needed for improvement and the detachment needed for patience?

In conclusion to the goal of meditation, I feel there is something few people talk about. What happens if you can sit and face all the disturbances of your mind and you reach a long period of time where little irritates you? Your mind is very quiet and peaceful. Imagine what this is like; it is a mind full of nothing and everything. There may be nothing magical in this peaceful state; it means you are simply at peace with where things are in your life and in the world, while simultaneously fully playing your role in life.

Twenty-Two

Contentment

Human Doing versus Human Being

"I can't find the time to meditate" is one of the most common problems for the average person working on meditation. I also often hear: "Nothing is happening, maybe this meditation is a waste of time." Or, "I feel guilty... I'm just sitting here, getting nothing accomplished."

These are all signs of a society that measures a person on what they do and accomplish versus how they accomplish what they do. It is the old quantity versus quality discussion. A person who owns a nice car and big house is commonly described as "doing well." Over time, these types of external measures of a person's worth become internalized. For example, even a nonmaterialistic person can measure success by the number of people served. "We served a thousand meals to the homeless this weekend, it was a great success."

In meditation, the same "human doing" person measures how good she or he is at meditation. This thought process backfires because the thoughts in the mind are multiplied in intensity and frequency by the internal self-judging or self-criticizing process. "Wow, you're really doing a good job meditating, no distracting thoughts other than me praising myself…"

Childhood Programming

It is almost completely accepted to pat a little boy or girl on the back when they get a good report card. But in the process, pride is equated with external accomplishments; the child is learning to receive love by their efforts and not by just "being themselves." This may sounds strange—who wouldn't want to bolster a good student? An alternate method of honoring the good student (mind you, this example is speaking not to your child, but to your inner child, the part of you who remembers being a child) is to ask the good student what they learned and what they did to achieve such good grades. This will allow the child to identify with the process of learning and learn from the experience. The same approach can be applied if the good student arrives home with a lower grade. This way both students are motivated, and neither penalized. Another option for engaging a child is to say, "Wow! You must have learned a lot this school report period. What did you enjoy learning the most?" The child goes on to tell you about the latest lesson in great detail. An engaged conversation ensues. The child feels cared for because the adult actually listens and honors the child for who he or she is, not for what he or she does.

You may say such things to yourself after a meditation session filled with very few thoughts (good student) or a meditation session where your concentration was fleeting (bad student). Over time, you will realize that you benefit from both types of meditations and that good and bad are relative terms.

Honoring of One's Self

Notice how you do things and what you enjoy about the process. Notice that you accomplish more by enjoying the process. Notice that if you enjoy the process, burnout will not occur and your creativity will actually increase in the long run. Meditation processing is a perfect time to practice honoring the process of being a human being versus a human doing.

EXERCISE 1: DAILY PRIORITY LIST

Most of us have a set of internal beliefs that dictate our behavioral choices. In your journal, jot down your list of duties along with the underlying beliefs associated with behavioral choices. For example, one man was a dedicated parent and company man. Surprisingly, upon retirement, he became completely self-centered. This man had the belief that while working, a person had a plethora of responsibilities; at retirement, all those responsibilities would be lifted. This is an extreme example of diverse behaviors but proves the point that underlying beliefs dictate behavior. Beneath his work beliefs was the idea that working years were to be hard and retirement was to be easy. This belief was ingrained for years. In terms of meditation, this man would have an equally difficult task finding time for meditation during his working years. Conversely, it may appear that meditation would be possible after retirement. However, the more *laissez-faire* approach to retirement would resist any disciplined activity. Remember, what you do today is what you will do tomorrow; the thought patterns continue to make a loop; hence, enlightenment is for the moment.

By understanding your beliefs, you will be able to hold those beliefs lightly and adapt to best reach a state of inner peace while living in harmony with others and fulfilling realistic responsibilities.

1. List your priorities and perceived duties.

2. List the belief of each duty.

3. Examine the roots of each belief.

4. Decide whether the belief is relevant.

5. Revise your list and start again at step 1.

EXERCISE 2: THE BUCKET LIST

This is a powerful exercise that has been made more famous in recent films. Make a list of things that you wish to do before dying; the things you want to accomplish before you "kick the bucket." This may be things as grandiose as climbing the pyramids in Egypt to volunteering for underprivileged youth. You may wish to forgive someone from your past or even write a book about your experiences.

1. Write your bucket list.

2. After each item, write the feeling you would have after completing that activity.

3. Reevaluate the item from an objective point of view to see if the reason for that event is truly going to bring you and others contentment.

4. Share these deeply held thoughts with a friend or a counselor to verify your conclusions. (Be careful not to daydream during this exercise.)

EXERCISE 3: MEDITATION PRACTICE
ON "WHO AM I TRULY" SELF-INQUIRY

Recall from chapter 15 that the great Indian saint Ramana Maharshi often counseled students by teaching that self-inquiry would provide a solution to all of the student's problems. He promoted the practice of self inquiry particularly of repeatedly asking the question, "Who am I?" It is fine to begin the exercise writing in a journal. Ask this question until you exhaust all of your perceived ego notions, for example: daughter, mother, friend, worker, parent, gardener, cook, cleaner, meditator, lover of movies, from this place, and so on. Keep asking the question at any time. See what emerges. What do you discover? As you near your true self, the question stops and so do the thoughts. When you feel as though the response to the "Who am I?" question is beyond words, you are deepening your meditation.

Twenty-Three

The Value of Discipline

The Home Practice

For the charged topic of discipline, let us begin with personal reflection:

What does the word **discipline** feel like to you?

Please answer this with descriptive adjectives for emotions such as irritated, happy, tired, etc. Be honest, how does discipline feel to you as an adult? How did discipline feel during your childhood?

What words do you use in connection to discipline?

For example, do you say, "I have to meditate today?" or "I want to…", "I must…," or "I am going to…" Just as in spoken or written language, also in your mind: word choice is important and powerful! To be disciplined means that "I …" What words did you hear during your childhood?

How to you speak to others when they need to be more disciplined?

Do you sound like your parents? Do you sound meek or hesitant? Do you sound stern or controlling?

❋

Discipline is a charged word; charged with potential as well as with destructive patterns. Typically, the first connection to discipline occurs in childhood within the family dynamic around children looking after themselves. Hence, an understanding of your family of origin dynamic reveals your starting point. Most children hear discipline in terms of commands from an upset parent. Seated at a desk during school hours is the most common time for discipline experience to form. This creates resistance or further negative associations to discipline for many people.

Depending on your unique experience, most peoples' starting point with discipline begins with resistance. Dedicated people figure out ways to overcome the resistance but often use something like personal meditation time as an area to stray from structure. Adding another discipline to an already structured life with work and family responsibilities may feel overwhelming.

Ironically, when you love an activity that makes you feel good, there is no view of discipline because you thrive in the activity. As children, no one had to discipline us to play with friends or force us to listen to a story. As adults, no one needs discipline to enjoy hobbies like gardening, reading, or meditation. However, because meditation practice depends on repetitive practice on a daily basis, there are times where the force of discipline is needed to ensure continued progress.

The word *tapas*, discipline in the yogic sense, is associated with fire. One description states that only a spark is needed to start a fire; hence, discipline may be considered just enough energy to begin practice. Once in the practice, the discipline can be forgotten. Eventually, discipline as a spark may be experienced as a gift for performing activities which have a positive effect.

A common thread for meditation practitioners is the importance of peer support for motivation. If you plan to meditate for years to come, take time to figure out who may help nurture the fire of discipline with community support.

EXERCISE 1: PRACTICING LOVING-
KINDNESS MEDITATION TO YOURSELF

Mindfulness is the practice of paying attention moment to moment to what is (refer to chapter 14). Both on the cushion and in our daily lives, we train ourselves to direct our attention in four areas: the body, the feelings, the mind, and the emergence of wisdom. Mindfulness teaches us to suspend temporarily all concepts, value judgments, mental comments, and ideas about and interpretations of what we are experiencing. In essence, we let go of the "story" of what is happening and simply observe it happening. The purpose is to attend fully to the present moment without our habitual "filters" that can distort reality. We begin to gain clarity about our experience without our own chronic interpretations or socially conditioned ways of being. As we develop practice both on the cushion and in our daily life, insight into the nature of reality arises.

1. Meditation relates to psychological development, whereas often what we think applies only to pushing thoughts aside.

2. Extirpate every thought or feeling you have with loving-kindness.

3. Next, think of those who give you resistance, and greet them with loving-kindness.

4. It may take time to forgive, accept, and shower them with loving-kindness.

5. As you continue in an unstructured fashion, go back to greeting your thoughts and feelings with loving-kindness.

Twenty-Four

Self-Study

Accepting the Future
with Vision and Patience

Thoughts about the future can be a big distraction for meditation practitioners. The daydreaming temptation looms with each meditation session. You may worry about the future or simply obsess on how your life could be better. Once the train of future thoughts begins, it can derail an entire meditation session without the practitioner even noticing. To help with this process, try the following exercise to concretely think about your future. This lesson's goal is to understand a constructive direction for your life to allow a deeper acceptance.

EXERCISE 1: REFLECTING ON YOUR "BUCKET LIST"

1. Review your "Bucket List" (from chapter 22) by outlining all the things that you want to do before you die. Be outlandish, even if the first round of the list may be unrealistic: Climb

the Himalayas, start a school, win the lottery, sail around the world, experience nirvana, or open a meditation center.

2. Next add to the list simple items, like spending every Sunday with family or planting a vegetable garden.

3. Take one list item and ask yourself what you will gain as a human being after that experience. What will scaling Mount Everest give you? For example: "It will be an experience of freedom, being so high on the earth in such a holy land, or a sense of accomplishment and vigor." Continue this process with each item.

4. Looking at the key priority topics, focus on the essence of each point and remake the list in a more realistic fashion but in a way that will allow you to experience the event's inner aspect. For example, I may not scale the Himalayas, but I would like to go camping somewhere very remote to experience profound silence in nature.

The point of this revised "Bucket List" helps quell unrealistic fantasies while allowing the essence of those experiences to be expressed in your life. Understanding your deeper desires can help remove the worry or fears of not doing something. Likewise, it is a reminder that you are complete right now just as you are. To further understand your life purpose to create freedom of mind and a solid vision, try the following exercise.

EXERCISE 2: BACKWARD PLANNING

The ancient Japanese art of archery teaches an exercise of shooting an arrow by tracing back the steps to the final result. The archer first sees the arrow in the bull's eye, and then he follows the flight course arc that the arrow travels. Before that, he studies the physics of archery. The archer sees how the bow is aimed and held, he notices the breathing, posture, strength, and concentration of the master archer. In training, the archer takes each of these phases into mind. Let's apply this backward planning procedure to your personal life. We'll start at the end of life and journey backwards.

EXERCISE 3: "WHEN I AM 100 YEARS OLD..."
There really are no rules for your experience here. Close your eyes and imagine yourself at a hundred years old.

- Can you see your physical self?

- Can you allow that image to emerge?

- Do you see yourself in a particular place or environment?

- Are you alone or with others?

- What is the larger spiritual purpose of your existence?

- Where do you live?

- What is your diet and overall daily routine?

- What is important to you?

- Who *are* you at this point; what is your essence?

Complete this exercise in your journal by answering similar questions for your forecasted self at age 65 (if you have achieved the wise age of 65 or greater, skip this line and follow the general instructions to follow). Sequentially, continue to answer the questions in ten-year increments until you reach five years older than your present age. In a more detailed version, write what you will do in the next five years to grow into that content hundred-year-old. Write down what the hundred-year-old version of yourself would need to do in the present to arrive at that enlightened version of your self.

For the final step, write down how you spend your time at your present age. Be honest with everything you do. Write down the pressures you feel and any negative behaviors in which you engage. This will give you a spiritual "to do" list so you can begin exploring what practical steps are necessary for your life as you have forecasted it. When you plan backwards like this, you will realize what you need to be doing in the present in order to reach the future goal. Keep these categories in mind (though this list is by no means exhaustive): relationships, work, study, spiritual practice, exercise, nutrition, finances, location...

As circumstances change in your life, you may update this exercise's findings. The goal is to know a direction for your life and therefore feel at peace while meditating. By understanding the process of your life as it unfolds, you will be directed. Then, you will be free to meditate without needing to worry about your future because you'll have a direction and realize that the future is actually right now.

Twenty-Five

....

The Meaning
of Surrender

Yielding to a Higher Reality
via a Beginner's Mind

Peace of mind collides with the usual motivations in a capitalistic society. Capitalism uses competition to motivate workers. This same competition may be internalized such that you think you must meditate without any disturbance and meditate without disturbance by the end of the week! A perfectionist attitude perplexes the meditator—the harder you try to be quiet, the louder the mind says, "Be quiet already!" Imagine calling your mind to attention but the mind does not respond for a year. You might resort to yelling, "Quiet mind, quiet now!" This overexertion only makes sitting still intolerable, if not uncomfortable.

The desire for simple peace of mind also inhibits practice of a focused mind. Each time you think, "I want peace," your mind thinks again. It is a paradox that we achieve peace of mind when we relinquish needing the peace. That is why meditation teacher Thich Nhat Hanh titles a book *Being Peace*. When you "be" peace, you are still. You are not trying to be peaceful, nor are you wishing to have it. You simply learn how to "be peace."

Another intellectual detriment is cleverness: those who know much have excessive thoughts and find it harder to reach stillness. You may know all the techniques of meditation and still not be able to practice properly. Shunryu Suzuki, a Zen meditation teacher, aptly describes the concept in his book *Zen Mind, Beginner's Mind.* "In the beginner's mind there are many possibilities, but in the expert's there are few" (Suzuki, 17). The meditation expert remains open-minded. To actually meditate, one transcends the ordinary capacities of the mind by quieting thoughts. Skillful meditation practitioners realize that no one human being's knowledge can encompass the universe. The open mind understands deeply by observing the spirit of each moment.

The paradox is illustrated as somehow the thinking mind must train itself not to think. This process occurs in varying levels over time. A few key components:

1. The mind behaves differently throughout your life.

   During this meditation process, you have discovered new aspects about how your mind works. Deep healing may occur and actual changes in your personality may take hold. The insights you have gained will remain with you. More insights await you in the future.

2. Expect the unexpected.

   The workings of the mind are complex, and no one can predict what is going to happen next in a person's life. Soothsayers may indicate potential future events, but there are no absolute predictions about the future beyond expecting the unexpected. Keep an open mind.

3. Remember that your reactions to situations create the next thought.

The saving grace in the midst of the mysterious process of quieting the mind lies in the power of your reaction to your thoughts. The way you greet distractions sets the stage for your future thoughts. Approach thoughts with a calm sense of understanding and the thought following the disturbing thought will be a calming thought. If you learn how to respond to all of your thoughts with tranquility and wisdom, your overriding experience of life will be more joyous. This type of awareness allows for accepting life's unexpected events as well as for the various changes that occur within your mind.

EXERCISE 1: MEDITATION ON SELF-OBSERVATION

Simply practice the final point of responding to your thoughts from a spiritual perspective. Sit quietly and use any meditation style or practice that suits your personality. Then, when the first thought enters, greet it with acceptance. For example, if the mind starts thinking about a worldwide ecological disaster, greet the disaster with acceptance. If you think about your body, accept it. If you have no thoughts, accept that too. In your own way, practice a simple response to the activities of your mind. Feel supported in knowing that even the most experienced meditation practitioners have thoughts. The difference with an experienced practitioners is the ability to respond with peace.

Part V

*Resources
Along the Way*

This section lists resources for continued growth after the foundation for a meditation practice has been established. A set of guidelines for finding a local class are listed. Meditation groups for each of the six meditation types will be listed (websites and contact information). This cannot be a complete list, but it will be a useful starting point for the reader's own research. An annotated bibliography of key books for each type of meditation is also provided.

Twenty-Six

Tips for Finding and Joining a Meditation Group

For thousands of years, meditation has been practiced in group settings. As the human mind is very complex and plays tricks on even the most adept practitioner, it is most supportive to join others for your practice. While this book has been guiding you in discovering your personal type of meditation, sharing the space for practice with others can have profound impacts both during meditation and when you are away from your cushion. Those living in urban areas will usually have a greater selection to choose from, but even if you live in a more rural area I encourage you to join a group, even if it is not exactly the type that you have explored in this book. Being with others and sharing the joys and struggles that accompany meditation is a key ingredient. Nothing can replace the positive effect of sharing your inner experiences in a safe setting.

Fictional Case Studies Exploring Meditation Group Classes

Following are several fictional case studies that summarize the possible extremes that can frequently occur with the different types of meditation.

In other words, the case studies show elements that may exist in varying combinations. Each meditation group is different, as is the personality of the group's leader. Rather than have you be turned off from meditation classes, I would alert you to be careful of some trends I have noticed in my years of training, and to do your best to seek out the positive, all the while knowing that each situation contains value for some people.

There exists a natural tendency to promote what works for you. Meditation groups promote themselves or encourage their students to feel that their tradition equals or exceeds another tradition. While it is very much in our nature to wish that our life experiences be affirmed by others and that we assume when we find something that works for us it will work for everyone, this attitude can cause myriad problems. Though some groups might make these claims however, it does not diminish the effectiveness of their programs. The greatest problem is that there are six major ways of meditating, and each of these six categories has a multitude of varieties. This multiplies into literally hundreds of meditation styles and thousands of programs. For the beginner with access to the Internet or hard copy resources of meditation books, it can be very confusing and intimidating to a find a meditation practice to suit their type. It is my great hope that you have narrowed the field and know what you are looking for after experimenting with your temperament throughout this book.

Case Study 1: Scientifically Proven Meditation Practice

Mainstream meditation programs need to rely on science to convince the establishment of their effectiveness. Medical doctors believe science and will only recommend something that has been found scientifically to lower blood pressure and decrease factors that contribute to anxiety and depression. These programs are very clinical and precise, much like a prescription. Like standard medical care, the programs are usually expensive to offset the high rent of the corporate location or to pay the facilitators who are highly trained.

Pros:	This is a fine system for those who have a very analytical, scientific mind
Cons:	Those who are more heart-centered and/or religious may find this type of meditation to be impersonal or clinical; however, a caring teacher brings warmth to the clinical setting
Level:	Good for beginners due to extensive, in-depth instructions
Personal Attention:	Depending on the specific program, this style can be exceedingly good if an individual teacher is assigned to each student; it can be quite weak if the group is very large, however
Community:	Depends on the specific program, but as above, a small size can have a very solid community feel
Cost:	Tends to be extreme in either direction: high-priced for a specialist or free community offerings

Case Study 2: Eastern Master's Program for Enlightenment

This presentation offers the special once-in-a-lifetime chance to be in the presence of an enlightened Eastern meditation master draped in beautiful, traditional robes. No fees are charged, only donations of charity are accepted. The room is filled with flowers: an elevated dais and numerous enthusiastic volunteers have formed a welcoming community based on the master's teachings. People of all walks of life are accepted. The rooms are adorned with soft meditation pillows on the floor and sturdy chairs for those who require back support. Soft, spiritually engaging music lilts in the background as incense breathes an aura of peacefulness and tranquility in the humble room. Some practitioners are seated, eyes shut and breathing deeply.

The group meditates in communion and afterwards people recount having intense spiritual experiences. Thereafter, a much smaller number continue to meet weekly for meditation practice.

Pros: For those who honor the "guru" or saintly figure as a means of inspiration, this method can be very transformative

Cons: Some individuals will view this as religious fanaticism in the form of meditation; it may not resonate due to personal beliefs

Level: Intermediate, some established self-disciplined is required

Personal Attention: Could be none or could be in the form of group follow-up meetings

Cost: Typically donation only

Case Study 3: Prayer and Meditation at Your Local Place of Worship

"Pray to quiet your mind" was the message of a religious leader who inspired large audiences to quiet their minds by praying to God. In so doing, this leader gained support from the clergy as he was building membership and helping people with the benefits of mind-quieting practices. This type of religious group may use the prayers from its tradition or offer cutting-edge adaptations for the particular faith. As the yogis of yore say, "faith in God is the quickest path to the divine." The yogis state this because the intensity of the believer's faith carries the power to overcome superficial desires. In other words, a person can meditate on his or her deepest values to achieve a quiet mind.

Pros:	Deepens the religious person's belief and under standing of his/her religion
Cons:	Not accessible for the agnostic or atheist
Level:	Beginner with prayer; advanced would be termed contemplator
Personal Attention:	Depending on the group, may range from none to a close-knit religious community
Cost:	Based on the religious group, some sort of dues and possibly a (typically low) meditation course fee

Case Study 4: The Exclusive and Expensive Program

The slick marketing program lured those interested in meditation by its secrecy: "Learn the famed meditation technique thousands of people have tried!" No more information is given beyond the riveting testimonials that are indeed sincere. Perhaps you have heard of a friend who claimed that one system or technique was above and beyond all. That friend followed the program religiously for years with great results. You may not have a clue of exactly what they do, but it must be good to be such a secret! The fee is up to five times the price of the scientifically-founded meditation, but in return one is given private consultations. Of the thousands of people who spend thousands of dollars on this system, it works very well for a small number of people—worth every penny for those few people.

Pros:	The high cost causes many people to value the meditation practice more than if they learned the same simple practice in a less intense setting; this can be worth it; motivation is an important quality

Cons: Very expensive and may create a sense of success
                        based on a technique alone

Level: Beginning to advanced

Personal Attention: Exclusive meeting with the important person

Cost: Two to three times any other program; the most
                        expensive

Case Study 5: *The Unemotional,*
Nonpressuring Superior Method

Another donation-only supported method of meditation, this group
attracts an intellectual following. This type of practice tends to thrive
near universities or centers of the high arts. The members have tremendous emotional control and there are very few instructions aside from
being aware of your thoughts during the practice. There are many books
available that make complete sense on this particular meditation path.
Overt conversion of members is absent: members know one another's
faces but not the details of their lives. The aura of sophistication makes
this form of meditative awareness seem like it is for the experienced
mind. This system works very well for a small number of people.

Pros: To the point, focused; consistent space for
                        meditation practice

Cons: Not as friendly as other groups for those who
                        appreciate emotional support

Level: Intermediate

Personal Attention: Very little, unless there is an introduction
                        for beginners

Cost: Low cost

Case Study 6: Meditation Class at Your Local Night School

Nearly every town that has an Adult Learning School at a university or public school offers inexpensive evening courses on meditation. Many people experiment with these lower-cost programs to discover what meditation is. This safe entry into the practice expands the accessibility of meditation. However, there can be very inexperienced instructors in these programs as well as overly-qualified, retired professor types. Typically, however, one form of meditation is practiced by an enthusiastic instructor.

Pros: Short, assessable courses for experimentation

Cons: Inexperienced instructors; short courses with little follow-up

Level: Beginner

Personal Attention: Very little to none

Cost: Low cost

Case Study 7: Meditation Retreats

Retreat programs have the potential to be life-altering experiences. Isolated from one's daily routine, a level of personal freedom and insight may be supported. The leaders are typically well-trained, experienced, wise, and caring. The audience that is attracted offers knowledge and good fellowship.

There can be fanaticism or peer pressure to join a group at times, so research carefully before joining a program. However, because the programs are usually at least two days in length, learning from a different tradition can be very inspiring. This type of experience is cultivated by seasoned meditators who are established in personal practice. They benefit from seasonal to yearly visits in an inspirational setting. For beginners, the key is to establish a follow-up support system upon returning home in order to maintain the uplifting experience.

Pros:	Profound new experiences may occur and new perspectives or insights may dawn in the retreat environment
Cons:	Can be overly intense or biased
Level:	Beginner to advanced
Personal Attention:	Intensive during the retreat; no follow-up at home
Cost:	From donation-only or low cost religious organization retreats to high-priced New Age retreat centers

Case Study 8: Meditation for Your Type

Meditation for Your Type does not have one technique at the exclusion of all others; it incorporates all the styles. This method spends a tremendous amount of time first preparing the mind for meditation. Like a few of the above methods, it recognizes that a simple and focused lifestyle is necessary to secure twenty to thirty minutes a day for undisturbed meditation practice. This system stresses self-understanding and positive thinking. It teaches breathing, relaxation, and sensory mastery as very important to give meditation a chance to work.

This system funnels people to each of the established meditation traditions that may help them once they find their personal styles. All members leave this program with clear direction and instructions to share how others may find the meditation practice that works best for them.

Pros: Helps a person establish a foundation and find a path

Cons: Not the best for the long term; more of an introductory path

Level: Beginner to intermediate

Personal Attention: Very high; group support is a key to meditation practice

Cost: Average to higher for a formal course; average for ongoing classes

Resources for *Meditation for Your Type*

Retreat Centers are an excellent way to deepen practice: You may simply use Internet resources to find a retreat near you on the type of meditation that interests you. A general site that supports a very exhaustive list, www.retreatfinder.com gives you many options.

Websites are too numerous to list. Please use resources via the Internet to find groups referenced in the books.

Bibliography

This is a partial list of meditation books. If you see a tradition that is not mentioned, please forgive us. This book assists beginners in finding the type of meditation that suits their personalities. I encourage you to seek out places to visit and learn more about the various meditation traditions. There are more traditions than listed; this just gets you started.

Meditation Overview Books

Goleman, Daniel. *The Meditative Mind*. New York: G.P. Putman's Sons, 1988.

Monaghan, Patricia, and Eleanor Diereck. *Meditation: The Complete Guide*. Novato, CA: New World Library, 1999.

Buddhist Meditation

Rahula, Walpola. *What the Buddha Taught*. New York: Grove Press, 1959.

Thera, Nyanaponika. *The Heart of Buddhist Meditation.* York Beach, ME: Samuel Weiser, 1965.

Buddhist Mindfulness (Vipassana, South East Asia)

Gunaratana, Bhante H. *Mindfulness in Plain English.* Boston: Wisdom Publications, 2002.

Nhat-Hanh, Thich. *The Heart of Understanding.* Berkeley, CA: Parallax Press, 1988.

————. *The Miracle of Mindfulness.* Boston: Beacon Press, 1975.

————. *The Sun My Heart.* Berkeley, CA: Parallax Press, 1988.

————. *Transformation and Healing.* Berkeley, CA: Parallax Press, 1990.

Rosenberg, Larry. *Breath by Breath.* Boston: Shambala, 1998.

Buddhist Zen (East Asia)

Herrigel, Eugen. *Zen in the Art of Archery.* New York: Pantheon Books, 1953.

Suzuki, Shunryu. *Zen Mind, Beginner's Mind.* New York: Weatherhill, 1970.

Watts, Alan W. *The Way of Zen.* New York: Vintage Books, 1957.

Contemplative Inquiry

Easwaran, Eknath. *The Upanishads.* Petaluma, CA: Nilgiri Press, 1987.

Osborne, Arthur. *The Collected Works of Sri Ramana Maharshi.* York Beach, ME: Samuel Weiser, 1997.

Vivekananda, Swami. *Jnana Yoga.* Mayavati, Himalayas: Advaita Ashrama, 1948.

Wu, John. *The Tao Te Chung.* Boston: Shambala, 1989.

Wu, Yi. *The Mind of Chinese Ch'an (Zen).* San Francisco, CA: Great Learning Publishers, 1989.

Healing Prayer

Bakken, Kennth L. *The Call to Wholeness.* New York: Crossroad, 1985.

Dossey, Larry, MD. *Healing Words: The Power of Prayer and the Practice of Medicine.* San Francisco: HarperCollins, 1993.

James, William. *Varieties of Religious Experience.* New York: Collier Books, 1961.

LeShan, Lawrence. *The Medium, the Mystic, and the Physicist.* New York: Viking, 1974.

MacNutt, Francis. *Healing.* New York: Bantam Books, 1966.

Merton, Thomas. *Contemplative Prayer.* New York: Doubleday Books, 1971.

Sanford, Agnes. *The Healing Light.* St. Paul, MN: Macalester Park Publishing, 1947.

Smith, Houston. *The World's Religions.* San Francisco: Harper, 1991.

Underhill, Evelyn. *Practical Mysticism.* New York: EP Dutton, 1915.

Mantra

Easwaran, Eknath. *The Mantram Handbook*. Petaluma, CA: Nilgiri Press, 1977.

———. *Meditation: An Eight-Point Program*. Petaluma, CA: Nilgiri Press, 1978.

Palmer, Gerald E. H., Philip Sherrard, and Kallistos Ware. *The Philokalia*. London: Faber & Faber, 1979.

Mindfulness (Western)

Kabat-Zinn, Jon, PhD. *Full Catastrophe Living*. New York: Delta Books, 1991.

———. *Wherever You Go, There You Are*. New York: Hyperion, 1994.

Tart, Charles T. *Living the Mindful Life*. Boston: Shambala, 1994.

Preparation Exercises and Lifestyle

Easwaran, Eknath. *Take Your Time*. Petaluma, CA: Nilgiri Press, 1994.

Yogendra, Shri. *Guide to Yoga Meditation*. Bombay, India: The Yoga Institute, 1983.

Visualization

Gawain, Shakti. *Creative Visualization*. Novato, CA: New World Library, 1978.

Redmond, Layne. *Chakra Meditation*. Boulder, CO: Sounds True, 2004.

Yoga Meditation (Breath, Concentration)

Aranya, Swami Hariharananda. *Yoga Philosophy of Patanjali.* Calcutta, India: University of Calcutta Press, 1963.

Robinet, Isabella. *Taoist Meditation.* New York: SUNY Press, 1993.

Satchidananda, Sri Swami. *The Yoga Sutras of Patanjali.* Yogaville, VA: Integral Yoga, 1978.

Vivekananda, Swami. *Raja Yoga.* New York: Longmans, Green, and Co, 1901.